5-Minute Messages and More

by Donald Hinchey

Loveland, Colorado

Dedication

To Gabby, P.J., and the Children of Our Father

5-Minute Messages and More
Copyright © 1999 Donald Hinchey

Credits
Book Acquisitions Editor: Jan Kershner
Editor: Debbie Gowensmith
Quality Control Editor: Dave Thornton
Chief Creative Officer: Joani Schultz
Copy Editor: Janis Sampson
Art Director: Kari K. Monson
Cover Art Director: Jeff A. Storm
Computer Graphic Artist: Pat Miller
Cover Designer: Colorforms Art Studio
Production Manager: Peggy Naylor

Library of Congress Cataloging-in-Publication Data
Hinchey, Donald, 1943-
    5-minute messages and more / by Donald Hinchey.
      p. cm.
    ISBN 0-7644-2038-0
    1. Children's sermons.   I. Title.   II. Title: Five-minute messages and more.
BV4315.H557   1999
252'.53–dc21   98-44914
                                                                              CIP

10 9 8 7 6 5 4 3 2 1   08 07 06 05 04 03 02 01 00 99

Printed in the United States of America.

Contents

Section 3: Living With Jesus

Introduction

The success of children's messages in the church points to a need to communicate the gospel in a way children can understand and be glad about. Our Lord Jesus invited the children to come to him (Matthew 19:14) and even challenged his disciples to be like little children (Matthew 18:3). The popularity of the children's message indicates that the church is taking our Lord seriously.

Just as the other books in the Messages for Children series have, *5-Minute Messages and More* moves children's sermons beyond the object lesson to a more interactive and involving model. Not only do children learn and grow, but pastors, teachers, and enthusiastic lay leaders can use these messages to lead the children deeper into God's Word. All that is required is a love for the Lord and his children.

In this book, *5-Minute Messages and More,* each children's message goes a step further. Based on church holidays, other special days, and common themes in the church, the messages are joined by these other components:

● A commentary section provides ideas for preaching and teaching to an adult audience on the same subject that the children experience in their messages. Such continuity in material will give parents and children common ground for learning and conversation.

● A Children's Active Message, which follows the Children's Message, leads the children to a different location for their own fun learning activity. The suggested activities last from eight to fifteen minutes and focus the children more actively and deeply on the topic for increased understanding.

● Leader Tips alert the leader to special circumstances to look out for or give additional suggestions to make the messages go even more smoothly.

● Fun Follow-Up Ideas, included with most messages, encourage the children to rejoin the adults and share with them what they did during their Children's Active Message. These ideas help children and adults alike make the connection between the worshipping and learning centers of the church's life.

So are these messages like children's church? Although the messages and activities are helpful additional resources for those who offer children's church, they can also be used in other ways. If children usually join their parents for church, you can occasionally—but regularly—invite children to join together for a Children's Active Message in a different location, perhaps during the pastor's sermon. Some congregations find that scheduling a Children's Active Message once a month allows the children a special treat on a regular basis and allows the parents an uninterrupted time of listening to the sermon. The Children's Message and Children's Active Message should focus on the same theme the adults are considering, but they're simpler in content and involve the child in hands-on activity.

You'll also find *5-Minute Messages and More* a helpful resource for these programs:

● vacation Bible school or extended Sunday school—Because the messages are simple and teacher friendly, churches of any size can organize a Children's Message team from parents and other interested adults and teens who would share responsibilities.

● camp—Camp counselors, pastors, and parents will find these messages perfect for a setting where adults and children learn and play together.

● midweek programs—A worship service, meal, and evening program would be enhanced; while the adults study Scripture, the children can learn, too!

Getting Started

Using the ideas in this book, coordinate Children's Messages with the themes the pastor plans to speak about. The pastor may use the commentary section of each sermon to connect the Children's Message to the sermon's theme.

Recruit

In order for Children's Active Messages to be a successful ministry, you'll need volunteers. Parents or young people who are willing to give up an occasional sermon are excellent candidates. There should be one coordinator, either a staff member or a dedicated volunteer, to establish a routine and let the helpers know what is expected. The coordinator could work closely with the pastor to harmonize the themes of the sermon, the children's message, and the activity.

Funds

While the messages found in this book are designed to be cost-efficient, there occasionally could be some expenses involved. For example, many activities require basic art supplies, which will require funding. It may be important to include the expenses in the regular budget.

Location

You may hold the Children's Active Message in a classroom, gymnasium, or other fellowship area, as long as it's large enough for all the children. It should also be located far enough away from the sanctuary to provide sound insulation but close enough so the children can easily come and go. Because the Children's Active Messages are quick and intense, avoid using a room with good carpet and furniture. An open space with tables where children can quickly move into place and complete a project is ideal.

How Often?

To keep the experience "special," ideally plan to do the Children's Active Message once a month. Children will especially look forward to their special days. If you have limited volunteer help, however, you might schedule quarterly messages.

Publicity

Because Children's Active Messages are a new idea, place signs in the church and notices in the church newsletter or the church bulletin. For example, a notice might say, "Children's Active Messages are coming! Following the children's sermon on [date], all children are invited to [location] for a special treat. They will experience an active, exciting children's message based on the pastor's sermon theme. Plan now to have your children be a part of the Children's Active Message!"

Follow Through

After the helpers clean up, the pastor, the coordinator, several helpers, and a team of parents might want to take a few minutes to evaluate the day's message with these questions:
● Was there a sufficient connection between the adult theme and the children's activity?
● Were the children involved?
● Was the activity appropriate for the time and space available?
● Were there enough materials for all the children?
● How can we improve the next experience?
The coordinator may want to keep a notebook to track the progress of the Children's Active Message.

Expand your children's ministry! Use *5-Minute Messages and More* as a resource wherever adults seek to teach their children to love Jesus. Our children, as part of the worshipping, learning, and serving community of faith, will grow in their love for their Lord!

Section 1:
Church Holidays

1. Waiting for the Lord (Advent)

Theme: Waiting

Suggested Bible Text: "I will wait for the Lord, who is hiding his face from the house of Jacob. I will put my trust in him" (Isaiah 8:17).

Commentary

Advent, the four-week season of Christmas preparation, has a character all its own. Too often in our commercial culture, Advent disintegrates into the "shopping days left until Christmas." We miss the powerful words of the prophets, their hopeful message that comes through the centuries to inspire us today. The traditions of Advent can be exciting for children and adults alike as we celebrate the "waiting in hope" that Advent proclaims.

Children usually associate waiting with disappointment. "I want it now!" is their—and often our!—cry in this age of instant gratification. But waiting gives us time to make all things ready for the Lord, who came at Christmas as a baby in a manger, who is coming again, and who comes to us each day as our source of life and love. When children learn the fine art of waiting, their pleasure in Christmas intensifies, and we adults get more time to share the endless mysteries of the season. During Advent we can help our children enjoy waiting, anticipating, and expecting the Son of hope.

Remember this year that Scripture tells us that not only good things, but also God's Son, comes to those who wait in hope.

Children's Message

Preparation: You'll need a Bible, a calendar, and an Advent wreath.

We have [number] weeks left until Christmas, and I bet some of you are getting excited. Why is it so hard to wait? Let the children respond. **We**

often want things *right now!* We think if we have to wait, we'll not enjoy something as much. **What do you have to wait for?** Let the children respond.

Hold up a calendar. **My birthday is** [date]. **That's** [number] **days away. How about you,** [two children's names]—**when are your birthdays?** Count on the calendar the days until the children's birthdays.

Let's see. Jesus' birthday, Christmas, is [number] **days away. That may seem like a long time, so what could we do to help us wait?** Let the children respond.

Waiting gives us time to trust and praise God. Read the Bible text. **During Advent, which is the time just before Christmas, we not only wait for Christmas, but also trust and praise God. Today during your Children's Active Message, you're going to make Advent wreaths.** Hold up an Advent wreath. **Advent wreaths help us wait because we use them to count down the time before Christmas; we also use them to praise God. With your parents' help, you can light a candle each night of Advent as you pray with your family and read Bible verses about Jesus' birth.**

Waiting for Jesus' birthday gives us time to thank God for sending his Son into the world. We have [number] **more days until Jesus' birthday, Christmas. How can we show someone each day how much God loves them?** Let the children respond. **How can we tell someone each day about the real meaning of Christmas: that Jesus was born into this world for us?** Let the children respond. **Follow our helpers now so they can show you how to make an Advent wreath for your home to help you and your family wait for Christmas and praise God.**

Children's Active Message

Preparation: You'll need a Bible, an Advent wreath frame with five candleholders for each child, five Advent candles for each child, live or plastic greens, trimming shears, florist wire, and baskets. Cut the greens into pieces that are long enough to encircle the wreath frames. Cut the florist wire into two- to three-inch pieces.

Have children sit at tables with the Advent wreath frames, and place a basket of greens at each table. Be sure several adults are available to help the children assemble their Advent wreaths.

Pick up a wreath frame, and trace the circle with your

Leader Tip

You should be able to inexpensively purchase either foam or wire frames for Advent wreaths at craft or church supply stores. Frames are generally available in a variety of sizes, from a smaller child's version to family size. Purchase candles to fit the holders. Also, while live greens are more symbolic of the life that came into the world at Christmas, you may want to use plastic greens for safety.

Leader Tip

Depending on how many children you expect to participate, you may want to have children create Advent wreaths from wire coat hangers and green crepe paper or tissue paper. Stretch and bend the coat hangers to form circular frames, and loop crepe paper or tissue paper around the frames.

finger. Explain to the children that just as the circle has no beginning or end, God has always been and will always be. Say: **During Advent, which is the time before Christmas, we praise God, who is so strong and is always with us.** Tell the children that the green branches remind us of life and that at Christmastime we celebrate the beginning of Jesus' life on earth. Remind children that Jesus was born to bring the gift of life to us. Say: **Jesus said, "I have come that they may have life, and have it to the full"** (John 10:10b).

Show children how to attach the greens to the wreath frames. Have the children place the greens on the base of the wreaths while older children or adults attach the greens with florist wire. Be sure to twist the ends of the wire so it won't cut children's hands. Then tell the children to put the candles into the wreaths' candleholders.

Say: **Each week as Christmas draws closer, you and your family can light another candle to remind you of Jesus, the light of the world. During the first week of Advent, light one candle. During the second week, light the first and second candles. During the third week, light the first, second, and third candles. During the fourth week, light all the candles. On Christmas Eve or Christmas Day, light the candle in the center of the wreath. This candle reminds us that we celebrate Christ's birth on Christmas.**

Remind the children that they should never use matches without an adult to help them.

Fun Follow-Up Ideas

Help one or two children carry their Advent wreaths to the front of the church. Say: **Let's see what our kids made to help them wait for Jesus' birthday.** Hold up an Advent wreath, and say: **Their Advent wreaths will help them count down the weeks of Advent in hope as they wait for the King!**

Invite children to explain the significance of the Advent wreath by saying: **Perhaps [name] can tell us what the wreath's circle reminds us of. Let's let [name] tell us what the green branches remind us of. Let's invite [name] to tell us what the lights remind us of. Can [name] tell us how to use the Advent wreath?**

Say: **I think our kids did a great job putting together these Advent wreaths, and I hope you can use them in your homes to remind you of the coming Savior!**

2. Sharing God's Love (Christmas)

Theme: Serving others

Suggested Bible Text: "For I was hungry and you gave me something to eat, I was thirsty and you gave me something to drink, I was a stranger and you invited me in, I needed clothes and you clothed me, I was sick and you looked after me, I was in prison and you came to visit me" (Matthew 25:35-36).

"The Word became flesh and made his dwelling among us. We have seen his glory, the glory of the One and Only, who came from the Father, full of grace and truth" (John 1:14).

Commentary

The ultimate message of Christmas is this: The mighty God of all creation humbled himself to come to us. He dwelt first in a manger, then in a humble home. Later he lived with common people, but he did very uncommon things. Finally Christ suffered and died upon a cross for us. We truly see God's glory when we see Jesus in the common places of life.

In the mad rush to wring nostalgia or good feelings out of Christmas, we can miss the more important reality that God is not far off but dwells in our midst, empowering and encouraging us to bring his comfort and love to the world.

Jesus makes the extraordinary promise that "whatever you did for one of the least of these brothers of mine, you did for me" (Matthew 25:40). Christmas is a time of special compassion toward the poor and victimized. While God's people carry on Christ's ministry of healing and love year round, we especially focus on doing Christ's ministry at this time of year. The Children's Active Message today will involve the children in reaching beyond themselves to act in compassion toward others. At a time of year when children are encouraged to get, we can encourage our children to give. That is, after all, what Christ Jesus, the child of Bethlehem, did!

Children's Message

Preparation: You'll need a Bible and pictures of people in poverty or in hospitals. The pictures should be large enough for kids to see from a distance.

Christmas is getting closer. Only [number] more days to go! How do you feel about Christmas coming? Let the children respond. **In the book of John in the Bible, we learn that it's good to feel excited and happy at Christmastime because Christmas reminds us that Jesus, God's Son, lived with us. Here. In this world.**

Hold up the pictures so children can see them. **I have some pictures of people who are waiting for Christmas to come, too. How do you think the people in these pictures are feeling?** Let the children respond. **Why do you think they feel that way?** Let the children respond.

Jesus came to live with us, and we need to share the good news of Jesus' love with others. Then they will know about him and can be happy. In the book of Matthew, Jesus tells us that we can give him a very special Christmas gift. Let me read to you what Jesus says. Read Matthew 25:35-36.

When we help clothe and feed and cheer people, we're actually giving Jesus a special present. That's why it's so good to remember the poor and sick and hurting in a special way at Christmas; when we care for them, it's as if we're caring for Jesus. How do you think you can help others this Christmas? Let the children respond.

During the Children's Active Message, you'll make Christmas cards for people who might be sad at this time of year. After the service today, we'll take your Christmas cards to [location] to let others know that Jesus came to live with us at Christmas. I bet that will make the people feel a little happier! You'll also think of ways to help people not only at this time of year, but all year long. Jesus came to us so we would share his love with all people.

Leader Tip

If you want children to deliver their cards to a hospital, nursing home, or shelter after this message, make arrangements with the agency, and recruit some drivers.

Children's Active Message

Preparation: You'll need brightly colored construction paper, markers, glue, children's scissors, decorations for cards such as stamps and stickers, and religious magazines that show the baby Jesus in a manger or that contain special Christmas greetings—"Christ is coming!" "Joy to the world!" and "Merry Christmas!" for example. Place the items on a table. Also make plans to deliver the Christmas cards to a hospital, nursing home, shelter, or correctional facility.

Have the children fold the construction paper in half, gluing pictures and drawing Christmas decorations on the cards. Helpers should particularly assist the younger children in finishing the project within the time available.

After the children have made the cards, have several kids share their creations with everyone. Talk with the children about how our love and gifts can make Christmas happier for others.

Fun Follow-Up Ideas

Have children hold up their cards. Read the inscriptions from several kids' cards. Comment on how these messages of God's love will make others happy.

Leader Tip

You may want to spell out Christmas greetings on newsprint for children to copy—"Jesus is coming!" "Merry Christmas!" and "God is with us," for example.

Leader Tip

As an alternative Children's Active Message, invite the children to help pack gift boxes to give to people in need. First, ask church members to bring small gifts to the church. For the activity, place the items on a table, and help children put them into boxes and decorate the boxes. Then have the children make cards with greetings such as "God bless you at Christmas and always! From the children of Grace Community Church."

As a Fun Follow-Up Idea, have the children take some of their boxes into the sanctuary. Then ask a few volunteers to explain who the boxes are for and what's inside.

3. The "Stars" Who Lead Us (Epiphany)

Theme: Sharing faith

Suggested Bible Text: "After Jesus was born in Bethlehem in Judea, during the time of King Herod, Magi from the east came to Jerusalem and asked, 'Where is the one who has been born king of the Jews? We saw his star in the east and have come to worship him' " (Matthew 2:1-2).

Commentary

Epiphany can seem like a real letdown after all the excitement of the Christmas season. But it doesn't have to be! Images of Magi, or wise men, from the East remind us that all nations have come to the Christ child. The maxim proclaims, "Wise men still seek him," and Epiphany encourages the seekers. But where is God raising stars for us to follow? What in our lives points the way to our Messiah, Jesus? The signs of God's guidance are all around us. His Word gives clear direction in times of ambiguity. God sets wise counselors around us—friends, pastors, and teachers—who provide guidance in times of searching. God doesn't leave us on our own but sets "stars" in our lives to lead us to his Son.

During the Children's Active Message, the children will think about the stars in their lives. Who are *your* stars? You might want to think, too, of who in your life God uses to guide you.

Children's Message

Preparation: You'll need a Bible; a large, brightly colored poster board star; and a marker.

A star led the wise men to Jesus. Hold up the star, and pass it around. **Bright and shining in the sky, the star led the wise men from far, far away to Jesus' home, and they worshipped Jesus when they found him. God**

used a beautiful star to lead others to his Son. Read the Bible text.

What or who does God use today to lead people to Jesus? Let the children respond. As the kids mention the "stars," write the words on the paper star. **God uses bright stars in our lives all the time to lead us to his Son. How do you think God can use you to lead people to Jesus just as the star led the wise men to Jesus?** Let the children respond.

In your Children's Active Message today, you're going to make some stars to remind us that God leads us to his Son. Why, God even wants to use *you* to lead others to Jesus!

Children's Active Message

Preparation: You'll need paper, markers, children's scissors, star patterns, a hole punch, and string. Set the items on a table.

Remind the children again of the star that led the wise men to the Christ child. Say: **God uses so many different people to help us find his Son. Who in your life has helped lead you to Jesus?** Let the children respond.

Help the kids trace or draw stars and then cut them out. Let kids decorate the stars and then write the names of those "stars" in their lives who lead them to Jesus. Encourage the children to draw pictures of their guiding stars. Help kids each punch a hole in one point of the star and thread the string through the hole.

After children have finished their stars, invite children to hold up their stars and talk about the people who lead them to Jesus.

Leader Tip

You may want to invite three costumed "wise men" to talk with the children about where they found Jesus, what he looked like, who his parents were, and how they found him. Once the children get into the spirit of the drama, *they* will be able to tell the wise men about their newborn King. A more expanded Magi encounter is printed in *5-Minute Messages for Children.*

Leader Tip

Depending on the number of children, you may want to further prepare some supplies ahead of time. Cut out a star for each child; then punch a hole in one of the star's points. You can also cut string into twelve-inch lengths.

Leader Tip

If picture church directories are part of your congregation's life, make the family photo sections available for kids to find their family pictures.

You could also send home a note with the children two weeks before you plan to do this message, asking Mom or Dad to send several family photographs for children to use. Be sure parents know that children will cut up the photographs.

Fun Follow-Up Ideas

Remind everyone that God uses many different people and circumstances to lead people to Jesus. Say: **As God used a star to lead the wise men, he uses "stars" to lead us. Family members, youth leaders, mentors, teachers, counselors, and others serve to lead others to Jesus.** Mention particular programs your church offers that provide such guidance. Say: **He also wants us to lead others to his Son.**

Ask kids to hold up their stars and tell about the guiding stars in their lives. Then ask children to tell who they think they can lead to Jesus.

4. Bearing the Cross (Lent)

Theme: Service

Suggested Bible Text: "Just as the Son of Man did not come to be served, but to serve, and to give his life as a ransom for many" (Matthew 20:28).

Commentary

Lent is the season of the cross.

The simple cross is the essence of what it means to be a follower of Jesus. Over the centuries, the cross has been decorated with gold and diamonds, placed on church steeples, and embroidered on banners and tapestries. Countless crosses adorn the necks of countless of God's children, many who may not even know what the cross really means. But understanding that Jesus' death on the cross is the vehicle of our salvation is basic to understanding what it means to be Christian! And yet we, as sinful people, sometimes want to avoid the cross.

It's nothing new. Jesus' disciples certainly wanted to avoid it. They often assumed that following Jesus would mean riches and rewards. In the book of Matthew, Jesus reminds his disciples that "the Son of Man did not come to be served, but to serve, and to give his life as a ransom for many" (Matthew 20:28). Jesus spoke these words shortly after the mother of James and John tried to get one of her sons a place of honor in Jesus' kingdom.

If the Son of God came to serve, why would we do any less?

The cross would keep us from self-serving. Its simple form reminds us of one whose desire to serve took him to a cross, a grave, and beyond to glory. Lent is the time to lift high that cross. A crossless Christianity is one in which there is only honor, glory, and pain-free discipleship, the very opposite of what Jesus commands for his church.

Lent is the time to look to the cross, the eternal sign of Jesus' servanthood, and to bear our servant crosses as well.

Children's Message

Preparation: You'll need a Bible and different kinds of crosses such as a plain brass cross, a wooden cross, a cross holding Jesus' body, a cross necklace, and a simple craft-stick cross.

In the Bible, Jesus talks of servants. Who knows what a servant is? Let the children respond. **Can you think of some people who are servants in your life?** Let the children respond.

How about you? Are you a servant? When do you serve others? Let the children respond.

Jesus tells us that being a servant is a wonderful thing. As a matter of fact, serving other people is what Jesus' friends do. That's what Jesus did, too! He served us in the greatest way of all when he died on the cross for us. Read the Bible text. **The cross is very important to us.**

Here are some different kinds of crosses. Pass the crosses around. Let kids hold and touch them. **Some are worn around your neck, others are hung in homes and offices. Where are there crosses in the church?** Let the children respond. **A cross with the figure of Jesus on it reminds us that Jesus suffered and died for us. If there is no figure on the cross, it reminds us that Jesus rose again. When we look at the cross, we know that Jesus suffered and died for us because he wanted to serve us. The cross can also remind us that Jesus wants us to serve others.**

Today in your Children's Active Message, you'll be making and decorating crosses. You can each wear your cross to remind yourself and others that you are one of Jesus' special servants!

Children's Active Message

Preparation: You'll need a Bible, craft sticks, markers, yarn, and scissors. Cut the yarn into two-foot lengths.

Help the children glue the craft sticks together, forming crosses. As the glue dries, read the Bible text again, and talk about the significance of Jesus' death on the cross. Remind children that Jesus came to be our servant especially by dying on the cross for our sins. Ask the children how they think they can serve others.

When the glue has dried, help the children write their names on their crosses. Then show children how to hold the middle of the yarn at the intersection of the craft sticks and crisscross the yarn a few times over the sticks. Finally, help children tie the two yarn ends together so children can wear their crosses around their necks.

Fun Follow-Up Ideas

Say: **Our servants are back! They have made such beautiful crosses to remind us that they are Jesus' servants. Would some of the children like to tell us how they think they can serve others?** Let the children re-spond. **Our church also serves others.** Describe some of your church's current ministry programs.

Say: **Lent is the season of the cross. Let's all look for ways to serve one another.**

5. The Hallelujah Puzzle (Easter)

Theme: Praise

Suggested Bible Text: "After this I heard what sounded like the roar of a great multitude in heaven shouting: 'Hallelujah! Salvation and glory and power belong to our God, for true and just are his judgments'" (Revelation 19:1-2a).

Commentary

Easter is the day of the great "hallelujah!" The word "hallelujah" means "Yahweh be praised."

Life for many Christians is an ongoing, ponderous rehearsal of sin and suffering. Some say the Puritans lived in constant fear that someone, somewhere, was having fun. Is it any wonder that the world is so suspicious of the Christian claim that true joy is found in Jesus when that message is delivered so joylessly? Easter is the high point of the Christian year and is also the apex of Christian joy. Can we think of any greater cause for joy than the resurrection of Jesus? In the empty tomb, Jesus triumphs over sin, the hopelessness of death, and the power of Satan. Because of his victory, our days on earth are marked with hope! We can rejoice! Our "hallelujahs" flow from our lips on this Easter day and live in our lives forever!

In the Children's Active Message today, we will invite our children to unravel a puzzle. As they put the pieces together, they will discover the message of Easter. It's a "hallelujah" puzzle that we can put together each day of our lives!

Children's Message

Preparation: You'll need a Bible, poster board, colorful markers, and scissors. Before the message, make several posters with the word "hallelujah" written in bright colors. Cut the posters into moderate-sized puzzle pieces. Also number the pieces and create a number key so the puzzles can easily be put together again. Hide the cut pieces of the puzzles in fairly obvious places around the room

in which children will be hearing the active message. If the we
the puzzle pieces outside. Keep one puzzle piece for the Childı

Hallelujah! Christ is risen! Have the children respond by
risen indeed!"

**Hallelujah! What a fun word to say. Let's say it together. Hallelujah!
The word means "praise God," and that's what we're doing today. Can you
tell me why?** Let the children respond. **What happened on the first Easter?** Let
the children respond. **Jesus rose from the dead on the first Easter. Because
he did, everyone who believes in him will live forever with God in heaven.
Let me read to you a verse from the book of Revelation in the Bible.** Read
the Bible text. **John, the man who wrote Revelation, says that someday when
we're all in heaven, we'll gather around Jesus' throne—and guess what
we'll be shouting.** Let the children respond with a loud "hallelujah!"

**But for now, our hallelujahs can get broken up and hidden kind of
like this little puzzle piece I have in my hand. On Easter, we remember to
shout "hallelujah" because we're so happy that Jesus rose from the dead.
When we get sad or angry or when we do things that make Jesus un-
happy, it's hard to sing our hallelujahs. They're all broken up. But on
Easter, we want to gather our hallelujahs again and make it whole—one
big, loud "hallelujah!"**

**During your Children's Active Message today, you're going to go on a
"hallelujah hunt." Let's see if you can find your hallelujahs this Easter.**

Children's Active Message

Preparation: You'll need to follow the preparation
instructions in the Children's Message section.

Say: **We've hidden the pieces to several puzzles.
Each puzzle spells out the word "hallelujah." Let's
hunt down the puzzle pieces and put them together.
Let's see if we can put together our big hallelujahs!**

Leader Tip

If the group of children is
large, different puzzles may be
hidden in different locations.
Send preschool children to one
location; first-, second-, and
third-grade children to another
location; fourth-, fifth-, and
sixth-graders to another
location; and so on.

When kids have found all the pieces, have kids return to the room to put the
puzzles together. Ask children if finding the pieces was difficult, and then let the children respond. Say: **Sometimes finding the hallelujahs in our lives is harder.
We can forget how much Jesus loves us and is always there for us. That's
why we need to remember Easter and Jesus' great victory. Let's shout a big
"hallelujah" now!** *Hallelujah!* **What's that? I can't hear you!** *Hallelujah!*

6. Up, Up, and Everywhere!
(Ascension Day)

Theme: Jesus' presence

Suggested Bible Text: " 'But you will receive power when the Holy Spirit comes on you; and you will be my witnesses in Jerusalem, and in all Judea and Samaria, and to the ends of the earth.' After he said this, he was taken up before their very eyes, and a cloud hid him from their sight" (Acts 1:8-9).

Commentary

"Where is Jesus?" We hear this question not only from children, but also from students and seekers in search of faith and from sufferers in search of answers. On Ascension Day, we specially remember that Jesus is everywhere! He ascended to the Father so that the Holy Spirit could be poured out on the disciples, who would then tell all corners of their world about Jesus. The point of Jesus' ascension is not to assure us that Jesus is "up there" in a far-removed heaven, but to remind us that although Jesus often seems incognito or hidden from our sight, he is nonetheless everywhere. Jesus reigns over our world. He is as close as the Word and is present in his body, the Church. It is the task of Jesus' disciples to share that good news with others.

Children often have an easier time believing in Jesus' constant presence than do many adults. Children can close their sleepy eyes at night and pray for Jesus' protection just as easily as they can talk to him at the dinner table and in the church pew.

So just as the children believe, let us all believe. We know Jesus by his wondrous acts, both in the past and in the present. He is always with us. Ascension Day is a good time to affirm that Jesus is everywhere!

Children's Message

Preparation: You'll need a Bible and a helium-filled balloon with a string long enough that you can let the balloon go but retrieve it.

Wouldn't it be great if Jesus had an office like your mom or dad may have? You'd always know where to find him. If you got locked out of your house, you could give him a call. If you were sick, you could send him a postcard.

Of course, there would be problems if Jesus had an office. So many people would want to call him that his phone would always be busy. You'd be kept on hold forever! And so many people would want to see him that you'd spend your whole life in line!

I'm kind of glad Jesus doesn't have an office. He doesn't need one! Jesus is everywhere!

On Ascension Day, we remember that Jesus returned to heaven to be with God. His disciples watched him disappear into the clouds. Read the Bible text. The Bible doesn't tell us what the disciples said as they watched Jesus rise up from earth. What do *you* think the disciples said? Let the children respond. I think the disciples must have been sad. First their best friend, Jesus, had died. Then he had come back to life. Then he left again.

Show children the balloon. Maybe the disciples felt like you do when Mom or Dad buys you a balloon at the circus or carnival and you forget to hold onto it. Release the balloon. Up it goes into the sky! What do you do when that happens? Let the children respond.

Then Mom or Dad tell you that you don't have to cry. Maybe they tell you that there will always be more balloons or that someone else will enjoy your balloon. That's the way it is with Jesus. There is always enough of Jesus to go around. He's never far away. He's in your home and your classroom; he's with you all the time.

How can we talk with Jesus all the time? Let the children respond. How can we tell Jesus how much we love him? Let the children respond. How can we share Jesus' love? Let the children respond. Jesus doesn't need an office. He has you and me to tell everyone about him!

During your Children's Active Message today, you're going to make some balloon bouquets to celebrate Jesus' ascension. Then you can remember that Jesus went up to heaven but really is everywhere!

Children's Active Message

Preparation: You'll need a tank of helium, uninflated balloons, balloon fasteners, yarn or ribbon, scissors, and colorful markers.

Leader Tip

You can rent helium tanks and buy balloons with string and balloon fasteners from most party-supply stores. Rental stores may also rent helium tanks.

25

Leader Tip

If you have a large group, you can fill some balloons beforehand.

As children enter the room, have the helpers begin filling balloons and attaching three-foot pieces of yarn or ribbon before passing out the balloons. Depending on the size of the group (and your budget!), each child may have two or three balloons. For each child, fasten his or her balloons together with a knot of yarn or ribbon.

Show the children how to decorate the balloons with markers, cautioning them that the balloons may break easily and cause everyone to jump! Help the children decorate the balloons with sayings like "Jesus is risen!" and "Jesus is here!" If balloons break, join in the laughter and replace the balloons.

When children have finished working on their colorful balloon bouquets, remind the children that we are happy today because Jesus is with us. Have them look for people with whom to share their joyful balloons.

Fun Follow-Up Ideas

Invite the children to show their balloons to the congregation and read what they wrote on the balloons. Say: **Balloons are happy symbols of celebration, and we have much to celebrate on this Ascension Day. Jesus is with us all the time, no matter where we are.** Invite the children to either keep the balloons or give them to congregational members to keep as reminders that Jesus is with them.

7. God's Spirit (Pentecost)

Theme: The Holy Spirit

Suggested Bible Text: "When the day of Pentecost came, they were all together in one place. Suddenly a sound like the blowing of a violent wind came from heaven and filled the whole house where they were sitting" (Acts 2:1-2).

Commentary

Pentecost proclaims, "God's Spirit is on the loose!" Jesus had promised that after he ascended to heaven, his Father would send his Holy Spirit to be with the disciples (John 14:26). It sounds calm and orderly, and yet the unleashing of the Spirit upon the disciples at Pentecost is anything but calm! The sound of wind roars through the upper room, and once-timid men become the vanguard of Christ's church. Who would have guessed?

Pentecost annually reminds us that the God who shocked the world with the resurrection of his Son at Easter continues to provide surprises aplenty throughout our lives. Just when we begin to think we're in control, a blast of God's Spirit whirls through our lives. Then we're reminded who really is in charge.

Bumper sticker wisdom proclaims, "If you want to make God laugh, tell him your plans." *God's* plans will ultimately show our petty agendas to be shameful. As we make our plans, can we add, "if God wills" in conclusion?

As surely as "the wind blows wherever it pleases" (John 3:8), so God will do his mighty acts where and when he pleases. Pentecost tells us that the Spirit of God is alive and well in the church, waiting to be used to advance God's kingdom.

Where do you feel the wind of God in your life? God's Spirit is ours for the asking. Let God blow mightily in your life!

Children's Message

Preparation: You'll need a Bible; one or two large fans; a few small, battery-operated fans; a pinwheel; a craft stick; several crepe paper streamers; and a stapler.

27

Before the message, staple the crepe paper streamers to the craft stick, and place the large fans so they'll blow on the children.

Today is Pentecost. It's "wind day" in the church. When the disciples were gathered in a room, not long after Jesus rose up to heaven, the sound of a mighty wind filled the whole house. Read the Bible text. **And that sound came from someplace special. Do you know where it came from?** Let the children respond. **Yes, the sound came from heaven. God's Spirit came at Pentecost like the sound of a mighty wind and filled the whole house where Jesus' friends were sitting. I bet that was fun, don't you?**

I'm going to make some wind today. Turn on the fans, and hand the small fans to older kids to turn on and hold. **Whee! That feels good. Where is the sound of wind coming from?** Let the children respond. **But even though the disciples in the upper room didn't know where the sound of wind was coming from, they knew what it was doing. It was filling them with God's love and good news so they could share God's love with everybody.**

The wind changes us. It gets us moving. Look at what it does with this pinwheel. Hold up the pinwheel, and let it turn in the breeze. **Let's see what happens when we hold up this streamer stick.** Hold up the streamer stick and let it blow in the breeze. **The wind really changes things, doesn't it?**

God's Spirit puts us to work for God. When we tell others about Jesus or when we serve other people as Jesus served us, then we're part of God's "Spirit Team." Let's all celebrate Pentecost by using God's Spirit in our hearts to serve him and work for him and tell others about him.

In your Children's Active Message today, you'll make Pentecost pompoms to celebrate the Holy Spirit.

Children's Active Message

Preparation: You'll need a Bible, eighteen- to twenty-four-inch wooden dowels, crepe paper, scissors, thumbtacks, and the fans from the Children's Message. Before the active message, cut the crepe paper into twelve-inch lengths. You'll need twelve lengths of crepe paper for each child. Set the supplies on a table.

Leader Tip

If the children are very young or if there are not enough adult helpers, have children use rubber bands to attach the streamers to the sticks.

As children arrive, have them sit at the tables. Read to them the story of Pentecost again, perhaps from a story Bible. Then invite kids to choose twelve pieces of crepe paper. Say: **There were twelve disciples, so we'll**

choose twelve pieces of crepe paper—one for each disciple. Have kids fan out the crepe paper streamers. Then have adult helpers use thumbtacks to affix the crepe paper to the sticks, making pompoms.

When children have finished their pompoms, turn on the fans again. Let the children wave their Pentecost pompoms in the wind! Then pray, reminding children that God's Spirit is in their lives all the time.

Fun Follow-Up Ideas

Arrange with the musician to welcome back the children with a lively praise song, or have the children sing, "If you're walking in the Spirit, clap your hands" to the tune of "If You're Happy and You Know It."

Have the children march into the church, waving their pompoms as the congregation sings. Then say: **What are we so happy about? It's Pentecost! God sends the Holy Spirit to help us serve him and the church. That's the reason for our celebration!** Sing a Spirit song to close the service.

Section 2:
Special Days

8. New Beginnings
(New Year's Eve and Day)

Theme: Celebration

Suggested Bible Text: "So teach us to number our days aright, that we may gain a heart of wisdom" (Psalm 90:12).

Commentary

The passing of a year offers us a backward and forward look all at the same time. As we remove the now-obsolete calendar, we recall times of joy and celebration with friends and family. There were birthdays and anniversaries that marked the passage of time in joyful, sometimes silly ways. But there were times of tears as well. Life is partially letting go, and the calendar reminds us of those times, too. Yet in all our times, God is with us. Every day and in each situation, God is here.

As we hang the crisp, new calendar, we wonder what the coming year will hold. What surprises will God bring to us? What burdens will we bear in these next 365 days? How might we wisely "number our days" in the new year, knowing that our days are not endless? As we are called to be stewards of God's good earth, so we are called to be stewards of our hours and days, receiving them as gifts from God and offering them back in joyful praise to our Creator.

New Year's celebrations invite us to remember that *this* moment may be the only one we ever know. How sad, then, is the expression "killing time." In time, we are meant to live life, find meaning, and praise God.

Children have a wonderful way of filling each moment with meaning. They explore their world with endless curiosity, savor their relationships, and raise the most fascinating questions about their God. May the childlike wonder never end. At this New Year's celebration, we'll invite our children to lead us in celebrating the God who guides all our days.

Children's Message

Preparation: You'll need a Bible and several noisemakers such as those described in the Children's Active Message.

Pass out noisemakers to some of the children, but ask them to wait until you tell them to make some noise.

Usually we tell our children to be quiet in church, but today I'm going to invite you to make some noise. You'll have to wait until I tell you to be noisy, though.

On New Year's Eve, people love to make some noise. Let's try! Let the children sound their noisemakers. **Why do people make noise on New Year's Eve?** Let the children respond. **New Year's Eve is a time to tell one another that we're excited about the passing of the old year and the coming of the brand-new year. We've had so much to thank God for in the year that's passing. Can you think of things about the old year that we can thank God for?** Let the children respond. As each child mentions something, have kids sound the noisemakers. **And what are you looking forward to in the coming year?** Let the children respond. As each child mentions something, have kids sound the noisemakers. **We want to shout "hip-hip-hooray" on New Year's Eve to praise our God, who gives us each new day. Listen to what the Bible says.** Read the Bible text. **When we "number our days," we remind ourselves that each day is precious. We can't put off praising God; every day is a great day to praise and serve God.**

On New Year's, we give thanks to God for the time he has given us— time for us to be together, to praise God, to love one another, and even to remember that someday time will end for all of us and then we'll live with Jesus forever!

How would you like to make a noisemaker like this? Hold up a noise-maker. **During your Children's Active Message, you'll do just that to welcome the New Year!**

Children's Active Message

Preparation: You'll need sample noisemakers and supplies for the children to make noisemakers. Try these noisemakers:

- oatmeal containers wrapped with construction paper, glued, and decorated
- rubber bands stretched over empty tissue boxes as "guitars"
- inexpensive party favors purchased from party supply houses that children can decorate with "Praise God Now!" and other phrases
- heavy construction paper rolled into a cone, taped, and decorated with "Praise God Now!" and other phrases
- pocket combs with tissue paper that can be used for humming a joyful hymn

Set the supplies on tables, and use the samples to show children how to make the noisemakers. As the children are making and decorating their noisemakers, remind children how important it is for us to see each day as God's gift. Say: **Our Lord blesses each day with his presence and wants us to unwrap it as a precious gift.**

When children have finished, let them try out their noisemakers. If you have time, have the kids sing a praise song while they keep time with their noisemakers.

Fun Follow-Up Ideas

Welcome the children back, and ask them to show you their noisemakers and describe them—but not play them! Remind everyone that we are so happy on New Year's Eve and Day because we're thankful for what God has given us and look forward to God's surprises in the future. Have the children wait quietly until you say, "Happy New Year!" and then let loose on their noisemakers.

Close by praying: **God of all our days, we thank you for all that you have given us in this year now passing and for all that is waiting for us in this year to be. Hear our prayer and grant us a "Happy New Year!" Amen.**

9. God Is Love
(Valentine's Day)

Theme: Love

Suggested Bible Text: "For God so loved the world that he gave his one and only Son, that whoever believes in him shall not perish but have eternal life" (John 3:16).

"Dear friends, let us love one another, for love comes from God. Everyone who loves has been born of God and knows God" (1 John 4:7).

Commentary

Ah, love! Valentine's Day is the day to find someone sweet and tell them you love them. For many children and adults alike, this day of remembrance falls into a bleak time of year; Christmas—a real feast of love—is long gone, and spring seems an eternity away. We need a day of warmth and light, and Valentine's Day perfectly fits the bill!

The kind of love to be celebrated on Valentine's Day varies. Parents and children lift up a love that is committed, comfortable, and close. Husbands and wives, sweethearts, and those trying to be sweethearts celebrate a more playful, tenuous love. But the common denominator to much of our Valentine's celebration is love as a "nice feeling." Lacy Valentine cards, sweet candy, and alluring colognes beckon us to get beyond our narrow lives of work and play and tell someone that we love them. A fine idea, to be sure.

Unfortunately, it can often end there.

What passes for love in our society can be more often a stirring of emotions than the committed covenant intended for human beings. It was that kind of covenant that God made with humanity in his Son. Paul's great "love chapter," 1 Corinthians 13, gives the details of this kind of love. It is Jesus' kind of love, and his cross is the supreme symbol for it.

When Christians send Valentine's greetings, they can remember the greatest "love note" of all—the Son of God, who died on the cross for our salvation. Valentine's Day can remind us to bring warmth and light to others through Christ's love.

Great men and women of our world leave behind various sorts of legacies. Buildings and books, fortunes and monuments all stand in mute, stark witness. Jesus, however, left love. A cross proved it, his Spirit shares it, and his disciples not only speak it, but live it. What a legacy!

Children's Message

Preparation: You'll need a Bible.

Soon it will be Valentine's Day. **What do we celebrate on Valentine's Day?** Let the children respond. **Who are some of the people you love? Who are some of the people who love you?** Let the children respond. **To be loved is a wonderful thing. It really is one of the most important things in life.**

I wonder who invented love. **Do you think two people were sitting together a long time ago and one of them said, "I think I'll invent love"? No, how silly! I'll read a verse from the Bible, and see if you can hear who invented love.** Read 1 John 4:7. **Who invented love?** Let the children respond. *God* **invented love. As a matter of fact, when God wanted to show us how much he loves us, he sent his Son, Jesus. Jesus died on the cross to forgive our sins and show us how wonderful God's love for us is!**

On Valentine's Day, we like to send cards to remind one another how important love is. But the greatest Valentine's greeting of all is Jesus.

During your Children's Active Message today, you'll have a chance to make a special Valentine for someone you love. That will remind both of you how much God loves you!

Children's Active Message

Preparation: You'll need colorful markers; paper; glue; and decorating materials to make Valentines such as lace, glitter, and ribbon. Set the supplies on a table.

Say: **Think of someone you really love. It might be Mom or Dad, Grandpa or Grandma, or a special friend. Using the supplies, make a special Valentine card for that person.** Suggest to the children that they write, "God loves you, and I do too!" on their cards.

As children work, reinforce that when we say, "I love you," we're sharing God's love. Stress the importance of showing love. That is, after all, what God did in sending his Son!

When children are finished, have volunteers hold up their cards, tell who they're giving the cards to, and why they're giving the cards to those people.

10. Fools for Christ (April Fools' Day)

Theme: Following Jesus

Suggested Bible Text: "We are fools for Christ, but you are so wise in Christ" (1 Corinthians 4:10).

Commentary

Stuffed shirts, the wise and pompous all get their comeuppance on April 1, the "feast of fools." The day provides opportunities for people to celebrate silliness and play harmless pranks and tricks on one another. In doing so, the element of surprise is introduced into routine lives, and we can affirm that we are not always as in control as we believe ourselves to be.

April Fools' Day reminds us not to take ourselves too seriously, which, after all, can be deadly. Work-driven men and women who focus only on their accomplishments and productivity may fuel our economy while they ultimately kill themselves and their relationships. Efficiency efforts would have us make every moment count. We're told to set visions, goals, and objectives, plunging ahead to produce. On the way, much of life's joy, beauty, and grace is missed.

Living as a Christian, Paul declares, means living by a "foolish" standard—a standard that doesn't make sense to the rest of the world. It all begins by confessing faith in a God who we cannot see but who involves himself with us daily and lovingly.

Christ's "fools" take direction from one whose Spirit infuses their lives with the foolishness of love, forgiveness, and hope. The cross of Jesus Christ is the ultimate "foolishness." God's forgiving love makes no sense to a world that lives by legalism. Christ's fools look for God's surprising intervention in life, and they are willing to share that vision with everyone around them.

Children's Message

Preparation: You'll need a Bible, a conical dunce cap with "I am a fool for Christ" written on it, and a harmless practical joke device—a buzzing ring or squirting flower, for example.

Happy April Fools' Day! For a long time, people have played tricks on one another on April 1. Show and demonstrate the practical joke. **Nobody seems to know exactly why, but April Fools' Day is a day to laugh and be silly. We can tell people we want to be silly by wearing funny hats, too, like this one!** Put the dunce cap on your head. **This is a way to tell people, "I'm foolish." How do I look?** Let the children respond.

Paul says the world thinks God's people are foolish. Read the Bible text. **Some people just don't understand how Jesus loves. "That's foolish," they say. Other people might think that forgiving others is foolish. Certainly following Jesus may seem to be very foolish to people who don't know about him.**

Today for your Children's Active Message, you're going to make a fool's cap like mine. What does my cap say? Let the children respond. **You can decorate your cap any way you'd like. Just remember, we are "fools for Christ!"**

Children's Active Message

Preparation: You'll need 8½x17-inch heavy paper, markers, glitter, tape, bells, and twine.

Remind the children that we can wear silly caps to let others know we feel foolish. Show children how to fold their paper to make a cone. Have helpers tape the caps in place.

Invite the kids to decorate their caps with markers, glitter, and twine. Help children print the words from 1 Corinthians 4:10—"Fools for Christ"—on their caps. Finally, to the tip of the cap, tape a piece of twine attached to a bell.

When kids have finished, have them put on their caps, march around the room, and sing a fun song such as "I Am a C."

Fun Follow-Up Ideas

Have a "fools' parade" in which the kids march into church, wearing their caps and ringing the bells at the tops of their caps. Have children gather at the front of the church, and then invite everyone to shout, "We are fools for Christ!"

11. Spring's Surprise
(Spring)

Theme: Growth

Suggested Bible Text: "See, I am doing a new thing! Now it springs up; do you not perceive it? I am making a way in the desert and streams in the wasteland" (Isaiah 43:19).

Commentary

Ah, spring. A time when signs of new life and growth are all around us. After the long, dark season of winter, the earth turns toward the sun, and the warmth of life floods our world.

No wonder that cultures throughout time viewed spring as an event as well as a season. It is a time of light for the human soul, a way of affirming that joy will triumph over sadness, hope over despair, life over death. As days lengthen, human beings affirm, often unconsciously, that the gift of life will lengthen and last beyond the final and greatest darkness—death itself. Spring celebrations throughout history have set feet dancing and voices singing in celebration of life.

God's Old and New Testament people have confessed over the centuries that spring is a year-round affair. Ours is a God who is forever renewing the old and bringing forth life from death. While many people focus on predictable seasonal changes, Jews and Christians can focus on the God who set the sun and stars in the heavens and who rolls this earth with clocklike precision. Beyond that, we lift up a God who will not stand apart from us, but involves himself in the affairs of people, setting us free to spring forth to life again and again.

Children celebrate spring by leaving behind the heavy, cumbersome coats of winter to frolic, sometimes prematurely, in the warmth of spring days. They easily make the connection with the new life that springs forth from the earth and the joy of an impending spring. God is working a "new thing," the prophet Isaiah promises. The earth whispers of God's renewing hand in life. Can we perceive it?

Children's Message

Preparation: You'll need a Bible and a collection of plants surrounding the message area.

Invite the children to sit in the circle of plants. **Shh, listen. Listen very carefully. What do you hear?** Let the children respond. **Put your ears to the plants around you. Do you hear them growing?** Let the children respond. **But can you** *see* **them growing?** Let the children respond. **Let's just sit here and watch the plants. When you can see one grow, hold up your hand.**

Hmm, the growth must be so slow that you can neither hear it nor see it. It's the same with some of you. I see you each week, and I don't notice you're growing. Then one day I look at an old picture or I see one of you I haven't seen in a while, and *wow!* **Have you grown!**

God slowly and steadily causes growth. God watches us grow and cares for us. Listen to what God told Israel through the prophet Isaiah. Read the Bible text. **God's "new things" are all around us in the spring. God is even causing growth in you which you can't see right away. But slowly, wonderfully, God makes us grow. God even causes growth within us. God sent Jesus to forgive our sins and bring us new life.**

Let's listen to our plants once more. Can you hear them grow? Let the children respond. **We still can't hear them, can we? Let's look at them very carefully.** Stare at the plants. After a few seconds, shake your head. **I must admit that I didn't see any growth. But that doesn't mean the plants aren't growing. In the few minutes we've been together, these plants have been changing and growing—just like you!**

Today let's thank God for giving us growth. In your Children's Active Message, you'll do some planting. Then, in a few weeks, we'll take a look at how our plants are growing. We'll do the planting, but God is making the growing happen.

Children's Active Message

Preparation: You'll need newspaper, foam cups or inexpensive flowerpots, small shoots of plants, potting soil, spoons, paper towels or hand towels, pitchers of

Leader Tip

It would be good to have some gardeners on hand to help with this message. In addition to aiding the children in the planting, they could provide some guidance on how the specific plants will flourish.

water, and markers. Before the active message, spread newspaper on the floor and tables where children will work. Set the supplies on the table.

When the children have gathered, say: **Today we are thinking of God's wonderful gift of springtime growth. How many of you have ever planted flowers or vegetables?** Let the children respond. **Today we're going to plant some** [name of plant]. **Then you can take the plants home, water them, give them sunlight, and watch them grow. The growth will be very slow at first, but in a few weeks you'll be surprised to see how tall your plants are getting!**

Help children each write their names on the bottom of the cups or pots. Then guide the children in carefully placing the soil into the cups or pots, gently covering the roots of the plants, and watering sparingly. As kids are planting, talk about the different ways God causes us to grow.

If you have time, have the children decorate their cups or flowerpots with markers. For example, children could write on their flowerpots these words from Isaiah: "Now it springs up!"

Fun Follow-Up Ideas

Invite the children to show their gardening handiwork to the congregation. Ask a few volunteers to tell a little about the plants and how children planted them. One of the children might pray, asking God to bless the plants and help them grow.

12. Remembering God's Truth (Memorial Day)

Theme: Truth

Suggested Bible Text: "But remember the Lord your God, for it is he who gives you the ability to produce wealth, and so confirms his covenant, which he swore to your forefathers, as it is today" (Deuteronomy 8:18).

Commentary

Remember! The commandment to remember echoes throughout the Old Testament and comes from a God who acted so vividly and decisively in the history of Israel. God gave the commandment to a nation with chronic memory loss. Every time Israel's identity as God's people was threatened, every time its very existence as a nation was threatened, the people met the threat as though it was the first they had faced. In response to their shaky faith came a call to strength: "Remember!" God had acted before, delivered before. God is stronger than any enemy. "Remember!"

The reminder to remember is not only for Israel. Despite the wise man's sigh, "There is nothing new under the sun" (Ecclesiastes 1:9b), we continue to believe that each challenge is unique, each obstacle is brand new, and each sin is original. Scripture tells us to remember. Remember that God has been present throughout human history—exacting judgment, building up, and renewing.

As Jesus faced the cross on the night he was betrayed, he lifted the Passover bread and cup and commanded, "Do this in remembrance of me" (1 Corinthians 11:24b, 25b). When Christians share the bread and cup, they remember God's suffering but victorious Son. Such occasions are a "Christian's Memorial Day," a time of bringing the past into the present. As we remember what God *has* done, we faithfully affirm what God *is* doing and *will do* in our future.

Children's Message

Preparation: You'll need a Bible, string, scraps of paper with notes written on them, your appointment book, some framed photographs of family members, and treats for the children. Before the message, tie a piece of string around your finger.

There is so much to remember! Remembering is very important, and God wants us to remember. Listen! Read the Bible text. **God wants us to remember the great and wonderful things he has done for us.**

So how do we remember? When you were little, your parents taught you songs that helped you remember. Let's sing one. Lead the children in singing the "Alphabet Song." **Then as you grow older, you're taught to write things down.** Show children the scrap paper with notes. **I carry an appointment book to remind me of important dates and things I must do.** Show children your appointment book. **We put up pictures in our homes and offices to remind ourselves of people who are important to us.** Show children the pictures. **Here's a trick we use to help us remember: We tie a string around a finger to remind us of something.** Show children your finger with the string tied around it. **Hmm, I forgot what I was supposed to remember! Maybe I'll think of it again.**

When we come to church, we come to remember. What do we remember in church? Let the children respond. **As we sing our pretty hymns, we remember that God is so great and we want to praise him. As we hear God's Word from the Bible, we remember the good things God has done for God's people in the past, and we know that God will continue to do great things for us. We so easily forget what a wonderful and loving God we have, so coming to this place of remembering is very important.**

Oh, I remember what this string is for! It's to remind me of the treats I brought for you today. Hand out the treats. **In your Children's Active Message today, you'll make some wonderful reminders for those who love you. And you'll share your treats as well.**

Don't forget to remember!

Children's Active Message

Preparation: You'll need good-quality paper with the words "Remember God's Gifts" and the date printed at the top and the words "Three Things I Like" on the side or at the bottom. You'll need one piece of paper for each child. You'll also need newspaper, crayons, paint that's easy to clean, soap, water, and towels. Before the active message, spread newspaper on the table where children will be working.

Say: **Today we have been talking about remembering. You children are growing up so quickly, and we thought it would be good to help your parents remember what a wonderful gift of God you are to them. Today you're going to make hand prints to give your parents. Our helpers will paint your hand and help you press it on the paper. As the paint is drying, please wash and dry your hands, and then come back to your place. We'll help you write your name and age on the paper and then three things you like.**

Have helpers help the kids use paint to make hand prints at the top of their papers. Then let the paint dry as kids wash their hands. After kids have washed their hands, ask the helpers to help the children write or draw at the bottom of the paper three things they like.

To close, have children stand in a circle with their papers. Say: **Let's say a prayer to let God know that we remember the good things he does for us.** Explain that you'll start the prayer, which will then make its way around the circle as children each name one thing from their papers to thank God for. When everyone has had a chance to pray, close the prayer.

Then say: **Now you can give your picture to your family as a reminder of what a gift of God you are to them!**

13. School's Out! (End of School)

Theme: Learning

Suggested Bible Text: "My son, keep my words and store up my commands within you. Keep my commands and you will live; guard my teachings as the apple of your eye" (Proverbs 7:1-2).

Commentary

The dismissal of school for summer vacation provides teachers and preachers with the opportunity to comment on education (and specifically Christian education) as a year-round phenomenon. In many communities, year-round schooling is becoming the norm as parents and teachers alike realize the effectiveness of continual, uninterrupted education. The concept of a three-month summer vacation from school hails back to the time when planting and harvesting required the help of children. In this age of technology, education can be a year-round affair!

The writer of Proverbs views acquiring wisdom as a lifelong process. Learning never takes a vacation, and the growth of God's people is perpetual. The charge to "keep my commands" was not so much a charge to observe a checklist of rules as a challenge to walk according to God's will throughout life.

Christian education is a lifelong process as well. Educators express justified concern that a generation of children are growing up without knowing the basic messages of the Christian faith. Many kids see the Bible as a mysterious relic rather than as the involving, timeless Word of God. Teachers who have committed themselves to lifelong Christian learning and who find excitement in their study will communicate that to children. Creative, interactive curricula will get the children involved in Scripture and its message and implant a hunger to know and experience more. As many students are dismissed from school for summer vacation, we in the church have an opportunity to stress the importance of continual Christian growth. Why wait until September to lift up Christian education? As we say "goodbye" to school for a while, we can say "amen" to lifelong learning.

Children's Message

Preparation: You'll need a Bible, some books from a church library, boxes, stacks of school books, pencils, rulers, papers, and other school supplies. Before the message, scatter the school supplies around the message area. Place empty boxes outside the circle of school supplies. Put a few books into a box. In the middle of the clutter, place a large Bible.

Invite the children to sit among the clutter. **School's out! How do you feel about that?** Let the children respond. **Summertime is the time to do things a little differently, and for many children and teachers, taking a vacation from school is one of the nice things about summer. Let's put these books and school supplies into boxes while I read a verse from the book of Proverbs to you.** Read the Bible text.

Continue when children have packed all the books and supplies. **That was good work, and we can get all those supplies out again when we go back to school. Even though it's summer vacation, I hope you don't take a vacation from learning. There is so much to learn and so many good books to read. Here, let me show some books to you. These are some books from a church library.** Show children the books. **Pick one up and look at it. What do you think you could learn from that book?** Let the children respond.

I wonder what we could learn from this book. Pick up the Bible, and let the children respond. **We could learn all about Jesus in this book. We could learn that God loved us so much that he sent his Son to suffer and die for us. There is so much to learn in just this book, the Bible, that we could spend years and years reading it and loving it.**

Listen to what the Bible says about learning. Read the Bible text again. **I hope that this summer you will continue to read all about God's world and especially about his love for us.**

In your Children's Active Message today, you're going to make a bookmark to help you with your reading. The bookmark will remind you that we are to keep learning about God all the time—even when school is out.

Leader Tip

If your church has a library, you might want to hold the Children's Active Message in the library. If you do, ask a church librarian or other teacher to acquaint the children with the resources available through the church.

Leader Tip

If the church is sponsoring a vacation Bible school, this would be a good time to invite children to attend and to hand out fliers for the program.

Children's Active Message

Preparation: You'll need 9x12-inch slips of tagboard, markers, crayons, string, and a hole punch. Set the supplies on a table.

Give each child a bookmark, and have the children write some of the favorite things they want to do this summer on the bookmarks. Help children write the words "Keep my commands" on their bookmarks, too. Have helpers punch a hole in each child's bookmark and then help the child tie a few pieces of string through the hole to make a tassel. As children work, the helpers should encourage them to keep coming to Sunday school this summer and to read throughout their days.

14. God Bless America (Independence Day)

Theme: Freedom

Suggested Bible Text: "Also, seek the peace and prosperity of the city to which I have carried you into exile. Pray to the Lord for it, because if it prospers, you too will prosper" (Jeremiah 29:7).

Commentary

National holidays like Independence Day allow us to reflect on the wonderful blessing of political freedom which citizens of the United States enjoy. We hurt as we watch television coverage from nations under despotic rule; the citizens' faces show fear and uncertainty. While we thank God for our freedom, we commit to keep our freedom alive and to support other's efforts to win that freedom in faraway lands.

Children who have grown up in a free society need to know the price of that freedom. Far from being merely a chance to celebrate, national holidays provide opportunities to instruct and remind one another about the lives lost and the sacrifices paid by those who served in the military and those who waited for them. We can never take for granted the freedom which we enjoy. Jeremiah's charge to "seek the peace and prosperity of the city" is timeless. If God's people don't do it, who will? Jeremiah's prophetic word to Israel is appropriate for us as well—"pray to the Lord" for the nation. That's the message for a national holiday!

Children's Message

Preparation: You'll need a Bible and a flag of the United States.

Soon we will celebrate Independence Day. Does anyone know what happened on the July 4, 1776? Let the children respond. **Our Declaration of Independence was signed. It is a very important piece of paper which says**

that our country is free. That's not the way it is in all countries. There are places in the world where people are told where they can and cannot go, what they can and cannot do, and even what they can and cannot believe. In some countries, it is against the law to gather for worship as we are gathered today. People can't work where they would like to or be with their friends or family. How would that make you feel? Let the children respond.

On Independence Day, we take time to thank God for our freedom. We can be with our friends and family, travel anywhere in this great country, and, best of all, we can worship our God.

Freedom is so important that on Independence Day, people celebrate! There are parades and picnics, and wherever you look, you see flags. Hold up the flag. It's a way of saying, "Hooray! We're happy to be living in the United States of America!"

The prophet Jeremiah had a very good piece of advice for all of God's people. Listen. Read the Bible text. "Pray to the Lord" for the nation. That's something we will do on this Independence Day, and you can help. In your Children's Active Message, you're going to make a copy of an American flag like this one; it can help you remember to pray for our nation this Independence Day.

Children's Active Message

Preparation: You'll need the flag you used during the Children's Message, white construction paper, markers and crayons, dowels, and staple guns with staples.

Hold up the flag, and point out to the children that the fifty stars stand for the fifty states of the Union. Have children name as many states as they can. Say: **The red can remind us of the men and women who have died to defend our country. The white can remind us that God wants us to be pure and love God. The blue can remind us that this country stretches from sea to shining sea under God's great blue sky.**

Leader Tip

If you're uncomfortable asking your helpers to use staple guns, bring sturdy drinking straws instead; have the children tape their flags to the straws.

Set out the white construction paper and markers, and have the children color the paper to make flags that look like the Stars and Stripes you brought. As the kids are coloring, have them sing patriotic songs such as "Yankee Doodle" or "God Bless America."

When finished, ask helpers to write the kids' names on the flags. Then have the helpers take the flags to an area of the room away from the children to use the staple guns to attach the paper flags to the dowels. When the flags are finished, have the children wave them. If you have time, have the kids recite the Pledge of Allegiance, too.

Fun Follow-Up Ideas

Arrange for the patriotic music to play as the children return. Children can march in a procession and wave their flags. Then children can lead everyone in reciting the Pledge of Allegiance.

15. Time for Fun (Vacations)

Theme: Renewal

Suggested Bible Text: "And a great crowd of people followed him because they saw the miraculous signs he had performed on the sick. Then Jesus went up on a mountainside and sat down with his disciples" (John 6:2-3).

Commentary

Throughout the Gospels, we're told that Jesus took concentrated time away from the routine of his work to commune with his Father and his friends. With vacation time upon us, it's good to reflect on the difference between what our culture calls recreation and a more biblical state of re-creation. The world's recreation can become "wreck-reation" with little effort. During vacations, we may frantically hurry from one campground or relative's home to another, grabbing fast-food meals while marking off sites on a travel map. When we structure our vacations as we do our workdays, marking off things to see and do, we can be assured that we will return home more exhausted than when we left!

Vacations can be—and should be—times of change to both our pace and our schedules. They can be times to reevaluate, asking ourselves whether the routines we have set for ourselves are really for our good. They can be times to try new experiences, stretching our tastes in food, music, and culture. Vacations can allow us time to see our loved ones in new ways without the pressures and expectations of routine. This kind of withdrawal creates an "oasis in time" where life can be examined and changes can be tried and discarded or kept.

Jesus set a wonderful example for us, withdrawing either by himself or with others to renew and refresh himself in communion with his God and Father. An examination of the Gospels reveals that either before a significant event or immediately following, Jesus "headed for the hills." He withdrew to a lonely place, often a mountain, to commune with God.

We might well follow Jesus' example. How might we use the vacation time before us to draw closer to God and our loved ones? Where might we seek solitude? How might we balance our vacation days with renewing, replenishing rest while seeking new adventures with our family and other loved ones? Vacation planning means finding that spiritual "mountain" that Jesus found and enjoying true, loving relationships with fellow disciples.

Children's Message

Preparation: You'll need a Bible, a travel map of the United States, and funny recreational hats.

Pass the hats out to the children as they come forward. Have different kids put on the hats. **The time of vacations is upon us. I know because many of you are missing from church on Sunday mornings, and I hope you're out in God's world doing different, wonderful, fun things.** Display the travel map. **Point out on this map the place you would most want to go on vacation.** Let the children respond. **What do some of you plan to do on vacation this summer?** Let the children respond. **Whatever you do, take some time to do what Jesus did on vacation. Yes, that's right—Jesus took vacations too. Listen.** Read the Bible text. **If you were Jesus, what would you do on vacation?** Let the children respond.

Jesus must have been very tired. He had been preaching and healing, letting everyone know about God's love. Jesus knew he needed time for his friends and for God. On our vacations, we can spend so much time running around that we'll come back home more tired than when we left if we're not careful. When we go on vacation, we need to remember to take time to rest and enjoy one another. We also need to take time to pray and give thanks to God for all he has given us in this wonderful world.

In your Children's Active Message today, you're going to make something to remind you and your folks to spend some time with God during your vacations. Let's go!

Children's Active Message

Preparation: You'll need inexpensive beach balls and permanent markers.

Set out the markers, and give each child a beach ball. Help the children write "Vacation With God" on their beach balls. Have the helpers assist younger children, encouraging them to decorate the beach balls with the permanent markers.

Leader Tip

You may want to have the younger children and older children form separate circles.

When kids are finished, have them stand in a circle. Say: **We're going to toss a couple of beach balls around the circle. When the ball comes to you, catch it and then say somewhere you'd like to go or something you'd like to do on your vacation. Say it as quickly as possible, and then toss the ball to someone else.**

Toss the first ball to someone. After that ball has been tossed a few times, toss in an additional ball. Continue until the kids are struggling to keep up with all the balls and the game has dissolved into laughter.

Fun Follow-Up Ideas

Let the children involve the whole congregation in the fun from their active message. Explain the game the kids played, and then have the kids toss their beach balls to the adults, who can then name places they'd like to go or things they'd like to do on vacation.

16. On your Mark, Get Set, Grow! (Back to School)

Theme: Learning

Suggested Bible Text: "After three days they found him in the temple courts, sitting among the teachers, listening to them and asking them questions. Everyone who heard him was amazed at his understanding and his answers" (Luke 2:46-47).

Commentary

It's not often that teachers find themselves *amazed* at a pupil's performance. But then Jesus was no ordinary student. His zeal for learning kept him from promptly returning from Jerusalem, causing great concern in his parents. (Can parents imagine how Mary and Joseph must have felt when Jesus did not return in the crowd from Jerusalem?) Jesus, like other Jewish youths of his day, knew that education was not a mere matter of memorizing facts and spitting them out. True education seeks to unearth the mysteries of life and the hand of God in our daily affairs. It is a constant wrestling with the ancient texts and the present situation.

If this was true for Jesus, how far greater the challenge for our young people! In a rapidly changing world, students are being required to master the latest in computer technology in order to understand the latest in scientific discovery. As students delve deeper into the complexities of the natural order, questions of life's meaning and the place of God in the universe can seem irrelevant.

So students returning to school face a wonderfully exciting challenge: Discover the details of math and science in order to use knowledge for the common good and for a greater understanding of God's will for humanity. We need to encourage students to study history and literature to see God's hand in the triumphs and tragedies of humanity. Can we infuse our students with an appetite for education that sees God's hand in all of the academic disciplines?

Too often parents fear that children's academic adventure will threaten their Christian faith. But with the support of faithful parents, teachers, and mentors, our students can unleash their God-given potential on learning about the world God has made. We can approach the new school year as the beginning of an adventure in which nothing less than the ways and wisdom of God will be discovered!

Children's Message

Preparation: You'll need a stack of books from various fields of study—math, science, literature, and history, for example. At the bottom of the stack, place a Bible.

It's back-to-school time! How are you feeling about that? Let the children respond. **Back-to-school time can be the start of a great adventure. You don't know what awaits you as you go back, but you can be sure that there will be a lot to learn. I brought some of the books you might be using in school this year, and each one has so many amazing facts. Did you know...** Open each book, and ask a child to read an "amazing fact." After each fact say, "Now, isn't that amazing?"

When the textbooks have all been explored, pick up the Bible and read the Bible text. **What was so amazing to Jesus' teachers was not that he knew so many amazing facts, but that he understood their meaning. I think Jesus knew that whatever we read about and learn in school tells us just a little more about this wonderful world God created. When we learn about the human body, it prompts us to praise the wonderful God who created us. As we learn to read better, we can read more about God's power and love. Math and science can teach us how God's world fits together so wonderfully.**

While many of you may not be reading much of the Bible in school this year, you will be learning about God's mighty works in creation. Pray that God will give you understanding to know that behind all of the world, all of history, all of you, is this great God who created the world.

In your Children's Active Message today, you'll think about Jesus' understanding and ask God to bless your new adventure in school this year.

Children's Active Message

Preparation: You'll need paper and crayons.

Have the children form groups based on grades—preschoolers, first through third grades, and fourth through sixth grades, for example. Ask adult helpers to help children draw and color pictures of Jesus in his classroom when he was their age. As they're making the pictures, ask them to think about what class was like for Jesus. **Do you think Jesus liked school? What do you think his best subject was? Why? If you were Jesus' teacher, what questions would you have asked him? If he were in your class as you begin school, what would he like best about your school? What would he like to change?** As the children reflect on their start of classes, help them to know that God will be with them in all they do and that whatever they learn will help them to better understand God's wonderful world. Close with a prayer, asking God for a great school year.

Fun Follow-Up Ideas

Have the children line up in front of the congregation. Invite their parents to join them, and say: **This week [or soon] our children will be going back to school. They'll have opportunities to learn more about God's world and how they might serve God. Today we want to give them our blessing as they go back to school.**

Proverbs 2:1-2, 5 says, "My son, if you accept my words and store up my commands within you, turning your ear to wisdom and applying your heart to understanding...then you will understand the fear of the Lord and find the knowledge of God."

As you go back to school, know that your God sends you on a very important mission. You will discover the wonder of God's world and the work God has done in the world through the years. You will find delight in God's gifts of art and music and words. Ask questions on your journey of discovery. Be curious! Remember that as you learn, you will grow in the fear and love of God.

Let us pray: Dear God, we thank you for these young people who will soon begin another time of education. Fill them with joy as they go back to school, and go with them into the classroom and the library. Accept the praise they give to you with their minds and bodies and all their gifts! In Jesus' name, amen.

17. Autumn Celebration (Autumn)

Theme: Death

Suggested Bible Text: "My times are in your hands" (Psalm 31:15a).
"You turn men back to dust, saying, 'Return to dust, O sons of men.' For a thousand years in your sight are like a day that has just gone by, or like a watch in the night. You sweep men away in the sleep of death; they are like the new grass of the morning—though in the morning it springs up new, by evening it is dry and withered" (Psalm 90:3-6).

Commentary

The passing of the seasons is a constant reminder of the rhythm of life. Spring is a time filled with promise, fulfilled within summer's lazy, languid brightness. Autumn is the time to remember that not all things are lasting; it is the time of the passing of life. As summer's growth fades through autumn into winter's sleep, we are mindful of the passages of our lives and of the glorious spring that awaits all of God's faithful people. Christians confess that God is Lord over all the seasons of our lives, involved in loving and often disciplining ways. Life is a purposeful journey through stages of divinely determined development. Even life's final season, which will culminate in our death, is in the hands of this good and gracious God.

Children need the occasional, sensitive reminder that life does not go on forever, but that God gives eternal life to everyone who believes in Jesus.

Children's Message

Preparation: You'll need a Bible and autumn leaves.

What a wonderful season autumn is! How do you know when autumn is upon us? Let the children respond. **This is the time of year when summer's warmth is going away and we're getting ready for winter's colder days. It's also a time to remember that God is in charge of all the seasons of our**

lives. How many of you like the summer season best of all? Let the children respond. **Let's have a big cheer for summer!** Pause. **How about spring people? Can you cheer for spring?** Pause. **Any winter people here? Let's give a big "brr" for winter.** Pause. **How about autumn?** Pause. **Each season has its own beauty, and we know that after fall comes winter, then spring, then summer. God is the God of all seasons.**

The Bible tells us that, just as creation changes and dies only to come to life again, all people will someday die. Read the Bible text. **It makes us sad to think of that, but we thank God that death is not the end of the story. Jesus died on a cross, and God brought him back to life again; God also will give eternal life to everyone who loves Jesus.**

Hold up the leaves, and pass them around. **Fall's autumn leaves remind us that death is a part of our lives, but we also know that spring will be here with more life again. Today in your Children's Active Message, you're going to make some pretty leaf pictures and thank God for the eternal life he gives everyone who loves Jesus.**

Children's Active Message

Preparation: You'll need leaves, paper of various colors and sizes, crayons, glue, cellophane, and tape. Before the active message, copy this verse on a large sheet of paper for children to copy or trace: "My times are in your hands" (Psalm 31:15a).

Leader Tip

If it is too late in the autumn season, leaves may be too fragile to glue or use for rubbings. You might instead invite the children to draw leaves and color them in.

As children arrive, have them sit at tables with leaves, glue, paper, and crayons. Remind the children that no matter what season it is, our lives are always in God's loving hands, and God gives us an eternal spring through Jesus' life, death, and resurrection.

First, ask helpers to help children write the Bible verse on a sheet of paper. Then show children how to make a rubbing of a leaf by placing a leaf under a sheet of paper and using the side of a crayon to rub the paper until you can see the shape of a leaf. Have children make leaf pictures on their papers by doing leaf rubbings and by gluing leaves directly to their papers. Finally, have helpers help the children tape cellophane over their leaf pictures.

57

18. God's Bounty
(Fall Harvest)

Theme: Hunger

Suggested Bible Text: "The eyes of all look to you, and you give them their food at the proper time. You open your hand and satisfy the desires of every living thing" (Psalm 145:15-16).

Commentary

This is the time of year when roadside markets proclaim the goodness of God. On crude wood shelving, the fresh produce is pinched, peeled, and carefully inspected before falling into brown paper bags for the trip to the home table.

It's hard to believe that in many nations, food is a scarcity. Drought, infestation, war, and the greed of those in power cause the land to withhold its bounty while people go hungry. What we take so for granted—that late summer and early fall will yield the richness of spring's planting—is a dream to much of the world's population.

When we give thanks to God for the earth's fullness, we also make a commitment to the earth's hungry. When sinful humanity stands in the way of feeding the hungry, it is time for the people of God to act. As we give thanks to the Lord, we ponder how we might share his goodness with others. The gathering of crops prompts us to seek ways of sharing such bounty with others.

Children's Message

Preparation: You'll need a "farmers" cap, a hoe, a shovel, a package of junk food, a few pieces of fruit, a few vegetables, and a collection of food described below.

This children's message and activity require preparation. Many churches are in partnership with community food banks that provide food for the poor. Several weeks before presenting this children's message announce that the church will be collecting food for the poor on that day. First, learn the needs of the food bank;

then ask members of the congregation to bring nonperishable food items to the church. Before the service, arrange a collection of the food donations where the children will hear the message.

Ask people to deliver the food to an area apart from the worship space. The children will assist adults in packing some of the food during the Children's Active Message.

You're all looking so good today, so healthy and full of energy. That tells me that you're getting some exercise and sleeping well. Being healthy means you're eating the right kinds of foods, too. A long time ago, the writer of one of our psalms praised God by saying, "The eyes of all look to you, and you give them their food at the proper time. You open your hand and satisfy the desires of every living thing" (Psalm 145:15-16).

What do you think that means? Let the children respond. **God feeds all people on earth so we can be healthy and enjoy a good life. God gives us such good food to eat. At this time of year, farmers put on their work hats** (put on the farmers cap) **and go out to the fields with their hoes and shovels** (pick up the tools) **and start to harvest some of the good food God has given to us. What are some of your favorite foods?** Let the children respond.

Even though God gives us such good food, do you know that some people eat real junk? Hold up the packaged junk food. **These taste good, and I must admit that every so often I like to eat some, but there are people who eat only junk food. What do you think will happen if all you eat is junk food?** Let the children respond.

God gives us fruits (hold some up, and give it to kids to hold) **and vegetables** (hold some up, and give it to kids to hold). **God gives us meat. God gives us food because he loves us and wants to see us healthy and happy.**

Did you know there are people who almost never have enough to eat? Our church and others like us collect food to give to those people. They ask God for food, and God gives them food through us! Jesus once said that when we feed someone who is hungry, it's the same as giving Jesus himself something to eat (Matthew 25:40). **What a great privilege we have in feeding people for Jesus!**

Your Children's Active Message today is very special. You're going to help package some of this food for people who are hungry. Then we'll pray that God will make them as healthy and happy as we are!

Children's Active Message

Preparation: You'll need boxes for the canned goods.

Have adults ready to help the kids in packing the food for the food bank. When the children have gathered, say: **While most of us have plenty to eat each day, many people in our town do not. So our friends have brought a lot of food for those people to eat. But they need your help in putting the food into boxes so it can be delivered. Let's see how much of this food we can put into the boxes so it can be delivered to the food bank.**

Remind the children as they work that all food comes from God, and they're acting on God's behalf in sharing food with others. When the time is drawing to a close, have the children stand around the packing boxes and offer a prayer of thanksgiving for all the good food God gives to us.

Pray: **Dear God, thank you for the food that keeps us healthy. Bless this food we have packed, and bless those who will receive it. Help us always to remember the poor and hungry of our town and world. In Jesus' name, amen.**

Fun Follow-Up Ideas

Invite each child to carry one or two cans of food and place them at the front of the congregation. Ask a few volunteers to explain what they did during the Children's Active Message, and then remind everyone of the importance of sharing what we have with others.

19. Voting Rights—and Responsibilities (Election Day)

Theme: Civic responsibility

Suggested Bible Text: "I urge, then, first of all, that requests, prayers, intercession and thanksgiving be made for everyone—for kings and all those in authority" (1 Timothy 2:1-2a).

Commentary

With national, state, or local elections drawing closer, we are reminded again that we are living in a nation where the very act of walking into a voting booth is a blessing. Not all people in the world are so fortunate! The process of electing officials who will work for their constituency may be cumbersome and complicated, but we do have the freedom to choose. The sad thing is that not all citizens choose to exercise that right.

Election day gives Christians the opportunity to reflect on what is important as we govern the affairs of state. We may vote for a candidate or slate of candidates, but in reality we are voting for values. How has their performance thus far and how will their promises promote what we believe is important for all the people? Will peace and a concern for life's holiness be advanced by their programs and promises? Will justice for the poor be furthered? Will proper stewardship of God's creation continue? When we pull a lever or push a button in a voting booth, we are putting our deepest values to work.

There are many who would set aside their individual obligation to inform themselves on issues and candidates by subscribing instead to a particular set of slogans and stereotypes. Marketing has replaced the lively exchange of ideas and convictions in the marketplace. Living as a Christian in the complex political world of the state has never been easy. Some dive in with such gusto that they are tempted to set aside their faith and ideals; then common good has been deprived of a faith-filled witness. Others have chosen to ignore such involvement entirely, but the consequences of political hermitage are dire! Witness the Nazi triumph that led to World War II.

Paul urged that "requests, prayers, intercession and thanksgiving be made for everyone—for kings and all those in authority" (1 Timothy 2:1-2a). Even though

61

the "kings and all those in authority" were most likely opposed to the Christian gospel, Paul recognized a citizen's obligation. Paul could not choose who would govern. Still he knew that the citizens' prayers were necessary. God hears and acts in ways beyond our understanding, and just because our candidate may not win, God will!

On election day, add a prayer to the act of pulling the lever in the voting booth. Pray that our leaders will seek God's kingdom and righteousness. All the rest will follow!

Children's Message

Preparation: You'll need a mock ballot showing the names of candidates in the election. On the back of the ballot, fill in the names of two of the children who will be at the Children's Message.

Election day is coming. People who are called candidates have been working hard over the last several months to convince us that we should vote for them. Who knows the names of some of the candidates? Let the children respond. **While children can't vote, you can look forward to the day when you can walk into a voting booth and vote for your candidate. That's a wonderful part of our freedom.**

Why do you think people want to be candidates in an election? Let the children respond. **When someone wants to serve in the government, they say they really want to make a difference in the way our country is run. They want to help people and want a better life for all citizens of our country. We thank God for people who want to be elected. Perhaps someday we'll see some of your names on our ballots.** Turn over the ballot. **Wouldn't it be great to have a choice between [name] and [name]?**

In your Children's Active Message today, you'll hold an election and see how we can best choose our candidates.

Children's Active Message

Preparation: You'll need cardboard or blankets, a chalkboard and chalk, white paper, markers, and tape. Before the active message, construct a large "voting booth" from cardboard or by hanging blankets in one corner of the room. Inside the voting booth, place chalk and a chalkboard with the names of the candidates running for public office.

Show the children the names of the candidates on the chalkboard inside the voting booth. Let them know that real voting booths are fancier than this! Talk with the children about the privilege of voting. Ask why they think people don't vote and why they think it's important that people vote.

Say: **We don't know who is going to win this important election, but we do know it's important to pray for them.** Read aloud 1 Timothy 2:1-2. Ask:

● **Why is it important to pray for our elected officials?**

Say: **Let's think about some prayers that we might offer to God for our country, our government, and our elected officials. I'll write them down on these pieces of paper, and we'll put them on our voting booth when we're finished.**

As the kids think of prayers, write them on the white paper; then post them on the voting booth. Then let the children take turns going into the voting booth to vote. Finish with a prayer for the country's leaders.

20. Thank You, God! (Thanksgiving)

Theme: Thankfulness

Suggested Bible Text: "How can I repay the Lord for all his goodness to me?" (Psalm 116:12).

Commentary

Why do we observe this holiday each year?

Certainly not because we need an excuse for gluttony or because it signals the beginning of the Christmas holiday season. Thanksgiving can easily degenerate into a hollow-day—merely another chance for change of schedule and excess of appetite—if we do not know who or why to thank. In rendering to the Lord our thanksgiving, we acknowledge that life, food, and indeed all our blessings come from the hands of a gracious God.

Whereas our culture would label us "consumer," one who *takes in*, Jesus stressed the role of human beings as "steward," one who *takes care of* that which is owned by another. We are stewards of this earth, caring for the possessions of God, who so graciously entrusts them to us.

God doesn't need our thanksgiving, but we need to thank! We need the annual reminder that we have been entrusted with so much and that God expects from us wisdom and compassion in allocating the bounty of this earth. Gratitude naturally leads to such stewardship.

How important it is to teach children the simple phrase "thank you." Children, too, can learn that thankfulness is an opportunity to celebrate God's grace and to be reminded of their responsibilities as stewards.

Children's Message

Preparation: You'll need a Bible and a piece of poster board with "thank you" written in several languages (see the following examples).

Spanish: Gracias (GRA-see-ahs)
Italian: Grazie (GRAT-see-ah)
French: Merci (MARE-see)
German: Danke (DAHN-ke)
Greek: Efcharisto (Ef-ca-REE-stow)
Aramaic (the language of Jesus): Shukran (SHOE-krahn)

Did you know that all people have their own way of saying "thank you"? When you travel in other countries, you need to know how to thank people. Let's have a language lesson in saying "thank you." Ask a child to hold the sign so it faces the congregation. Then lead the children in saying "thank you" in the different languages.

Now wherever you go in the world, you can thank people in their own language. Why is that important? Let the children respond. **We also need to say "thank you" to remind ourselves that we're depending on people for so much in this life. None of us can do everything by ourselves, so God gives us other people to help us. Also when we say "thank you," we remind ourselves that there are people we can help, too.**

We really need to say thank you to God, don't we? God is the One who gives us everything, and when we give thanks back to God, we're reminding ourselves of how much we need God. On Thanksgiving we will gather together to thank God for what God has done for us. Read the Bible text.

How does God take care of us each day? Let the children respond. **How does God use us to take care of others?** Let the children respond.

In your Children's Active Message, you'll get a chance to think of all the things we can thank God for and make a place mat for your Thanksgiving dinner. I can't wait to see what you will give thanks for.

Thank you **for coming to our children's talk. Danke!**

Children's Active Message

Preparation: You'll need colorful 8½x17-inch poster board, markers, stickers and other decorating supplies, magazines with brightly colored pictures, children's scissors, and glue or paste.

Leader Tip

If possible, use a laminating unit to put a protective covering over the completed place mats.

When the children have gathered, remind them that they're going to make place mats listing some of the things God gives us for which we give God thanks. Say: **God asks us to share** the many things we have. Let's think of some of God's blessings and draw them on the place mats. Can you draw a picture of your home? Mom and Dad? Your favorite food?

Have the children draw pictures, arrange stickers, and glue magazine pictures to their place mats. Help the little children especially, and have enough helpers handy to help cut and paste kids' thanksgivings on the place mats.

Fun Follow-Up Ideas

Have children hold up their place mats and explain why they chose or drew those pictures. Then lead them in a chorus of thanksgivings from around the world, using the poster board from the Children's Message. Close with this prayer of thanksgiving: **Thank you, God, for all the blessings you give to us. We thank you for those who take care of us and those we care for. Thank you for food, and help us to share with those who are hungry. Thank you for schools where we can learn and churches where we can praise you. You are such a great God, and we thank you for all you give to us. Amen!**

Section 3:
Living With Jesus

21. God Is Grace

Theme: Forgiveness

Suggested Bible Text: "Forgive us our debts, as we also have forgiven our debtors...For if you forgive men when they sin against you, your heavenly Father will also forgive you. But if you do not forgive men their sins, your Father will not forgive your sins" (Matthew 6:12, 14-15).

Commentary

Forgiveness is an attitude, an act, a way of life that finds its roots in the heart of God. It flies in the face of the human tendency to hold the grudge, exact the punishment, return tit for tat. In a society that cannot accept grace, forgiveness is a joke. What good does it do to forgive? How does that benefit *me?*

Jesus knows. Forgiveness is cruciform. It reaches to the heavens, into the very courts of the Lord; it also extends out to the neighbor whose sin has offended me, whose indiscretion slighted me, whose maliciousness wounded me. Forgiveness reaches both ways.

These words from Jesus' commentary on the Lord's Prayer are among the hardest in Scripture. Jesus means them to be. They are anything but simple, for our forgiving others does not motivate God to forgive us. My saying to you, "I forgive you," does not move God to cancel my debts. What moves God instead is the painful picture of his Son hanging on a cross whispering words of forgiveness for his executioners (Luke 23:34). No, forgiveness from God is not something I earn by offering my forgiveness, but it is accessible to me only as my heart is opened to forgiving others. To lock the gates of my heart from others and expect that God will come in the backdoor is foolish. When tempted to withhold forgiveness, either because I perceive the wound to be too deep or because I want a degree of control over another, is to close myself off from that free gift that God is placing before the front door. The key to unlocking that door is forgiveness.

Children's Message

Preparation: You'll need a Bible and a bowl of fruit.

This morning we want to talk about forgiveness. What is forgiveness? Let the children respond. **In the Bible, Jesus tells us to pray about forgiveness.** Read the Bible text. **When God wants to forgive us for what we have done wrong, he wants us to forgive others. As a matter of fact, we can't accept God's forgiveness when we're angry at others. Let me try an experiment with you. I want you all to close your hands as tightly as you can. Don't open them until I tell you to, OK? No matter what I do, don't open them. Ready?**

Hey, let's shake hands! Do you want to shake hands? You don't? Hmm. I've got an idea, let's wave at your parents. Ready? No? Hmm.

Now here's something special—a bowl full of fresh fruit. Tastes good, too. Want to get some? Just reach out and take it. Have the children finally open their hands. Share fruit with the children who would like some.

When we can't or won't forgive someone who has hurt us, it's like closing our whole selves up. We lock ourselves away from others, and we can't get the greatest gift of all—God's love in Jesus.

In your Children's Active Message today, you're going to do a play. That's right, a real live drama. And some of you are going to be the actors! Let's go now and learn more about forgiveness.

Children's Active Message

Preparation: You'll need five boxes about the size of a shoe box, one larger box, plain paper, tape, white paper, a marker, pretty wrapping paper, a small gift card, a pretty cross, scissors, and a note card. Wrap the five boxes in the plain paper (if they're plain boxes, you don't need to wrap them). Tape a small piece of white paper to each one. Then mark the first box with the word "anger," the second with the word "hate," the third with the words "no love," the fourth with the word "gossip," and the fifth with the word "pride." Inside the larger box, place a pretty cross with a sign that says, "I love you forever. Jesus." Wrap the larger box with the pretty wrapping paper. To that box, attach a card that says, "To all of my children on earth. Love, God."

Have the kids sit on the floor around an open "stage" area where the actors will perform. Tell the kids that you are going to tell them a story. Say: **I am going to make up some names, but I'll bet each of you knows what this story is about because we do this all the time. I need three actors to help me with the story.** Select three children to play the parts of Mark, Ryan, and an angel. It would help if the actors playing Mark and Ryan were outgoing "hams." Tell your actors that they'll need to act out the story as you read it. Say: **We also need five children to help by holding these boxes.** Select the volunteers, and tell them: **When I tell you, you'll put the boxes somewhere. Then later you'll take them back. Ready?**

Have the children act out their parts as you read the following story.

Once there was a very mean little boy named Mark, and there was a very nice little boy named Ryan.

One day Mark started a fight with Ryan and pushed Ryan down. Mark walked away, but then something strange happened. Mark found that he didn't like being mean, and he even felt sorry that he had pushed Ryan. So Mark went to Ryan, said that he was sorry, and asked for Ryan's forgiveness.

But Ryan had become very angry at Mark, and he held a great load of anger in his heart. Invite the child holding the "anger" box to come forward and place it in Ryan's arms. **He was so angry at Mark! Wouldn't you be?**

And the more Ryan thought about what Mark had done, his anger turned to hate. Invite the child holding the "hate" box to come forward and place it in Ryan's arms. **Well after a while, Ryan's heart had no love for Mark at all.** Invite the child holding the "no love" box to come forward and place it in Ryan's arms. **Ryan wanted everyone to know what Mark had done to him. He told everyone, and he even made the story worse than what had actually happened. He really enjoyed the gossip he was spreading around.** Invite the child holding the "gossip" box to come forward and place it in Ryan's arms. **And to make it worse, Ryan was filled with pride. He decided he was a lot better than Mark.** Invite the child holding the "pride" box to come forward and place it in Ryan's arms. **He would never, ever forgive that nasty Mark!**

Well Mark was very sad that Ryan wouldn't forgive him, and that was too bad. When God saw what was going on, he sent Ryan an angel with a very special gift. Invite the child holding the beautifully wrapped box to come forward. **The angel told Ryan, "All you have to do is take the gift, Ryan."** But Ryan couldn't take it. **Why?** Let the children respond.

The angel explained, "The gift is God's love for you. It's all for you. It forgives you of all your sins and promises that you'll live forever with Jesus—and it won't cost you a thing. It's a gift, remember! But I can't fit it over all those ugly things you've got in your life. How about putting them aside?"

Ryan thought and thought. He couldn't imagine walking around without his ugly packages, but they *were* getting heavy, and he couldn't see others clearly with them in his way. Besides, that beautiful package filled with God's love sure looked better. So Ryan let go of the pride (ask the child to retrieve the "pride" box), and he felt better. Maybe Mark was just like him after all. He didn't always do the things he should do.

And that gossip was silly! Besides, it only hurt others. So he stopped the gossip. Ask the child to retrieve the "gossip" box.

Plus Ryan was sad all the time without any love in his heart, so he let that go, too, and asked God to put love back into his heart. Ask the child to retrieve the "no love" box. As love filled him, Ryan noticed that hatred was leaving him. Maybe Mark was really not so bad a guy after all. Maybe he was just having a bad day. Ask the child to retrieve the "hatred" box.

And soon the anger seemed to melt away as love returned. Ryan felt lighter and happier. He saw other people as God saw them—wonderful children of God! Ask the child to retrieve the "anger" box. And for the first time in a long time, Ryan felt free! Now he could open the great gift from God. Have the angel hand the gift to Ryan. He invited Mark to help him. Invite Mark and Ryan to open the wrapped box after reading the card aloud. Then invite them to take out the cross and read aloud the sign.

And Mark and Ryan became great friends and lived happily ever after.

Discuss these questions with the children:
- Have you ever felt like Ryan?
- How are the feelings printed on the boxes like a big burden?
- What can we do when we feel that way?

Fun Follow-Up Ideas
Have the children perform the drama for the congregation. You can even involve more children by having a few volunteers ask the congregation discussion questions after the drama.

22. Love Letters

Theme: God's love

Suggested Bible Text: "God has poured out his love into our hearts by the Holy Spirit, whom he has given us" (Romans 5:5b).

Commentary

On a four-lane highway in the rural Midwest, there is a farm, old and obviously working. Nestled close to the intruding asphalt where countless cars speed by is a barn, again old and obviously working, with flakes of paint on gray, weathered board; a roof, slightly shingled; and two doors that meet more or less in the middle. Painted, faded red letters on the road side of the barn read, "God is love."

The message on the barn stands in stark contrast to the advertising signs up and down the highway. They're glitzy and sharply focused and sophisticated. "God is love" seems as obsolete as the barn it's painted on. Except that this barn has endured the decades, the storms, and the changes of a fast-moving society. Other billboards will come and go, and eventually the barn will collapse, but the message itself will live on.

That's the way it is with God's love. It endures in all of its simplicity throughout the ages. It's marked on barns and churches and signs and publications, but ultimately it lives through God's people. They teach it, live it, and pass it on to the next generation.

Preaching and teaching about the love of God is dangerous because it seems, at first, to be so trite. It is the sort of thing "religious" people are supposed to say. But let it sink in that we believe this world was created out of love. Consider that you and I are not the result of a chance meeting between sperm and egg, but are instead the precious children of a loving God. God's love is productive—it brings into being, redeems in such a costly way as a cross, and then nestles in the hearts of the beloved to be renewed and shared.

And all of that on the side of an old barn!

Children's Message

Preparation: You'll need a Bible; a trash can; and various kinds of mail such as bills, advertising fliers, solicitation letters, and invitations; and letters on nice stationery.

Every day when the mail comes to our house, there are different kinds of letters. Hold up the mail. **Here are some letters that say I owe money. Here are others that want to sell me something. Here are letters that want me to give some people money. Most of the letters I get in the mail go right here.** Drop letters into the trash can.

But there is one kind of letter I would never throw into a trash can. Show the children a letter on nice stationery. **This is a love letter, and it tells me that someone somewhere loves me. This is from my [relation]. Do any of you get any love letters?** Let children respond.

Love letters all have one thing in common: They close with the word "love." That lets me know that no matter how far away my loved ones are, they still love me.

I have one other love letter here. It's a big one! Hold up the Bible. **The Bible is God's great love letter to us. From beginning to end, it tells us God loves us so much that when the time was just right, he sent his Son to suffer and die for us. Why do you think God would do that?** Let the children respond.

Now I looked at the end of this love letter from God to find the word "love," but I found something else instead. Would you read it, please? Have an older child read the very last verse in the Bible. **That's just another way of saying "love," isn't it?**

In your Children's Active Message today, you'll write some love letters to others to let them know how much God loves them.

Children's Active Message

Preparation: You'll need pens, markers, paper, envelopes, and stamps. You'll also need a list of names and addresses of people in the congregation or community who are ill, hospitalized, or homebound.

Invite the children to select a name from the list and to address an envelope with the name of a specific individual. Help the younger children address their envelopes. When kids have finished, have them put postage stamps on the envelopes.

Then work with the children in writing "love letters." If the children are too young to write, adult helpers can be their "scribes." Suggest that the kids begin their letters with the sentence "Jesus loves [name]," and then fill in the names they've chosen. Encourage the children to save some space on the letter for artistic decoration.

When children are finished writing, help them sign "love" and their name. Then have the children decorate their letters and seal them. Tell the children how important it is to let people know that Jesus loves them. Have the kids stand in a circle. Close with this prayer, asking each child to fill in the name of the person they wrote a love letter to: **Dear God, thank you for loving us so much and for sending your Son, Jesus, to show us how much you love us. Please help our letters show these people your love.** When children have filled in all the names, end with "amen."

Fun Follow-Up Ideas

Have the children take their letters to show the congregation. Have a few volunteers explain what they wrote and the difference love can make in the lives of the people who will receive the letters.

23. We Have Gifts

Theme: The church

Suggested Bible Text: "Now you are the body of Christ, and each one of you is a part of it" (1 Corinthians 12:27).

"Consequently, you are no longer foreigners and aliens, but fellow citizens with God's people and members of God's household, built on the foundation of the apostles and prophets, with Christ Jesus himself as the chief cornerstone" (Ephesians 2:19-20).

Commentary

What a puzzle is the church! How a group of twelve students under the leadership of a carpenter's son from Nazareth could change the world defies logical explanation. And yet it happened and continues to happen. The sociologists examine the statistics of church attendance in the United States and predict a dark future for the church. But on other continents, the church is awakening from decades of dormancy or is stirring from the ashes of paganism. It is no mere sociological phenomenon, the church of Jesus Christ. It is his body, alive and well in the world.

The New Testament uses various images to describe the church: Christ's body (1 Corinthians 12:27), a holy temple (Ephesians 2:21), a spiritual house, and a holy priesthood (1 Peter 2:5). Today we're more apt to see the church as a local gathering of people or the building on Holly Street or some vast denominational structure. No one picture does justice to this complicated phenomenon that is the church of Jesus Christ. It is both intimate and global, as personal as the touch of one of Mother Teresa's nuns, as expansive as the sprawling "megachurches" that draw thousands for worship. A group of five Christians in a living room holding hands in prayer is the church. A gathering of thirty-five thousand screaming young people in a sports complex is the church. We are on the radio proclaiming the gospel; we are in the streets feeding the hungry and binding the wounds of the sick. Pipe organs and rock bands, steel drums and mariachi bands accompany our praise. But through all the diversity, magnificence, and mundane ministry, we can celebrate our unity, for we have been called by our Lord to be his church in the world.

Children's Message

Preparation: You'll need a Bible, a pen, slips of paper, a box, wrapping paper, scissors, and tape. On the slips of paper, write various personal gifts such as "the gift of piano playing," "the gift of singing," "the gift of kindness," "the gift of bringing joy," and "the gift of helping the church." Identify five or six people in the church who have these gifts, and ask that they be ready to demonstrate their gifts during the Children's Message. Place the slips of paper in a box, and wrap the box with wrapping paper. Be sure a child can easily open the box.

Hold up the gift-wrapped box so children can see it. **What a beautiful gift box. Let's see what's inside. [Name], would you like to open the box and show us what's inside?** Have a child open the box. **Let's see what the slips of paper say.** Read aloud the slips of paper.

Those are all wonderful gifts God gives his people. God gives each of us gifts, but they're not to be kept in a box. I bet there are some people here who have these gifts and can show them to us. [Name], I believe you have a gift. Would you show us how you share that gift? Have the person respond. **[Name], how about you?** Have the person respond. Repeat until all volunteers have shared their gifts.

Thank you for sharing your gifts with us today! God gives everyone such wonderful gifts to be shared right here in this church. The Apostle Paul calls the church the "body of Christ." Read 1 Corinthians 12:27. **Paul wants us to know that God gives us each gifts to share with the church.**

In today's Children's Active Message, you'll learn more about what it means to be the body of Christ. Think of the gifts God has given you. How can you share them with all of us?

Children's Active Message

Preparation: You'll need a Bible and masking tape. In as large a space as possible, use the masking tape to "draw" on the floor a large human form. Put the head at one end of the room, and create extended arms with fingers, a body, legs, and feet with toes. Draw a smile with tape, and use two small pieces to make eyes.

Ask the children to sit around the figure, and read aloud 1 Corinthians 12:27.

Ask the children what they see in front of them. Then ask:

● **Which part is the most important part of the body?**

Tell the children that in Paul's day, some people were confused about the church. Some thought they were unimportant people who didn't count. Say: **Paul used the example of the body to show us that we're all important and we all need one another in the church.** Ask:

● **If you didn't have a thumb, what difference would that make in your life? Can you imagine not being able to hear or speak?**

Then ask the children to think about the gifts that God has given them. Are they good in math or science? Do they play the piano well? Can they dance or run fast? Encourage them to see their abilities as gifts from God. Not everyone can do all things well, but each of us has special gifts to use in the church.

Point out that each of us has a place in the body. Invite kids to find a place on the masking tape body. Encourage them to be careful not to disturb the masking tape. Say: **If you're a good dancer or runner, find a place around the feet; if you're good in math or science, around the head. Are you a good listener? The ears are the place for you. How about singing or telling others about Jesus? You're "mouth people."**

When the children are in place, encourage them to see connections between the various parts of the body. The hands need the feet to get where they need to go. The head needs the hands to hold things or pick up things. Ears listen for the needs of others. We all need the heart to move us to serve. Help the children see the unity we have as Christ's body and understand that each member is needed.

Close with a prayer in which each section thanks God for their gift and commits to serving within the wonderful body of Christ.

24. I'm Hungry!

Theme: Caring for the poor

Suggested Bible Text: "Suppose a brother or sister is without clothes and daily food. If one of you says to him, 'Go, I wish you well; keep warm and well fed,' but does nothing about his physical needs, what good is it? In the same way, faith by itself, if it is not accompanied by action, is dead" (James 2:15-17).

Commentary

We are saved by God's grace through faith, not by our works (Ephesians 2:8-9). Yet James presents another perspective: This faith is an active, living faith that shows itself through works. We are not saved by works, but we are saved by faith for works. The distinction is fine but crucial, and no doubt hours could be spent in theological debate.

But James was only reminding us to do what Jesus did. While Jesus spent a good amount of time teaching and preaching, he spent a great deal of time healing and tending to people's basic needs. Feeding more than five thousand hungry people is no small task!

God presents to us the poor as opportunity rather than burden. Those who have so little allow us to show the love that we know in our hearts and speak with our lips. As society becomes more and more compartmentalized and isolated, our contact with the poor can be reduced to writing checks in the safety of our studies and praying in the quiet of our sanctuaries. The poor invite us into the streets.

When Jesus speaks of the last days in Matthew 25, he says he will separate his people not denomination from denomination, liberal from conservative, traditional worshippers from contemporary worshippers, but the sheep from the goats. The sheep will have been those faithful disciples who fed the hungry, visited the lonely, clothed the naked, and cared for the broken. In so doing, they will have ministered to Jesus himself! The goats will have had other things to do.

Thank God for the poor, who give us the opportunity to be Christ's sheep.

Children's Message

Preparation: You'll need a Bible and a banana. Before the message, ask three children to help you. Explain that you will be pretending to be hungry and will start to eat a banana. When you do, the children are to say, "I'm hungry! Please, can I have something to eat? Oh, I'm so hungry!" You'll continue to talk, and they'll continue to ask for food. When you put down the banana, they can stop their cries for food.

Good morning! Isn't this a beautiful day? What a wonderful day God has given us! I left the house so quickly this morning that I had no time to eat. I hope you won't mind if I have a little snack to keep up my energy level. Take out a banana, and peel it while the children you spoke with before the message say, "I'm hungry!" **Yes, it's very common to be hungry at this time of day. Your breakfast must be wearing down.** Eat some banana while the children complain. **You know, this banana isn't as sweet as some I've eaten. I wonder why.** Eat some banana while the children complain. **Now, now, I'm sure your parents will have some food for you later. Just don't think about how hungry you are—what a great banana!—and you won't even feel hungry.**

After a minute or so of this, fold up the banana peel and set the banana down. Tell the children that you and your helpers were pretending in order to illustrate a verse in the Bible. Then read the Bible text. **Can you be fed with words?** Let the children respond. **Of course not.** *Food* **fills people, not words. Once when more than five thousand people became hungry while listening to Jesus, guess what he did. He fed them! And he wants us to feed the hungry and care for the poor.** Mention opportunities that your church has for people to serve the poor.

Today in your Children's Active Message, you're going to learn how we can all help in caring for the poor. Jesus wants us to do that; when we do, we are truly blessed! By the way, I'll share my breakfast with all of you during the Children's Active Message.

Children's Active Message

Preparation: You'll need napkins, cups, fruit slices, juice, paper, and a pen. Set out the items on a table. You'll also need to ask a representative from a community agency to visit the church for the Children's Active Message. Explain that the children will be learning about feeding the community's hungry and that you'd like the representative to share some suggestions with the children about how they might help feed the hungry.

The children most likely will be a little hungry after the Children's Message, so feed them first! As they eat, ask them to think about what they feel like when they're hungry. Point out that in our world, there are children and adults who never have enough to eat. Then introduce your guest.

After the representative has shared information, invite the children to think of specific ways they might care for the community's poor. As they brainstorm, list their ideas on a sheet of paper. Then have the children vote by raising their hands and commit to either one more-involved idea or two or three smaller ideas.

Fun Follow-Up Ideas

Have several children tell the congregation about some of the ideas they discussed during the active message. Then have the children explain the idea they've committed to.

25. God's Spirit in Me

Theme: Self-esteem

Suggested Bible Text: "Don't you know that you yourselves are God's temple and that God's Spirit lives in you?" (1 Corinthians 3:16).
"Knowledge puffs up, but love builds up" (1 Corinthians 8:1b).

Commentary

Self-esteem is not pride. Pride is a subtle form of idolatry in which a person lifts up himself or herself to the point that God is seen as unnecessary or even a barrier to full potential. Pride sees no reason for God; prideful people don't think God can offer them any more than what they already have—even if they see their gifts as God-given.

Pride is isolating. My pride cuts me off from those around me who may need what I can give; pride feeds me the lie that I need nothing from anyone. It constructs an immediate barrier to correction: "How dare you seek to rectify me when I'm obviously so far superior to you!"

Pride is not a happy way to live. Isolated from God and one another, we grow further into ourselves, living constantly in a spiritual hermitage. God wants better for us. He wants us to live in community with one another and with him.

Now self-esteem is a whole other matter. Whereas pride creates a puffed-up picture of who I think I am, self-esteem gives thanks to God that I am his son or daughter. Pride is an exhausting pilgrimage in denial: "Certainly I cannot be wrong or rude, sinful or superficial. If you find me objectionable, then change your perspective!" Self-esteem recognizes that saint and sinner coexist within me but that God graciously forgives. (See Romans 7:14-25 for Paul's comments on his personal struggle.)

How do children learn self-esteem? Not through permissiveness. When children's poor behavior is not corrected because correction might hurt their fragile self-esteem, they only learn that nasty or careless actions are OK.

On the other hand, children learn of their value before God and others by consistent, appropriate praise; visible, tactile signs of love such as hugs and kisses; and constant reminders that they are created in the very image of God. Self-esteem acknowledges that while we can rebel against God and others, there will be consequences. However, self-esteem also acknowledges that God made us and loves us and won't cast us aside for that rebellion; instead, we can live within marvelous forgiveness for all our days.

Children's Message

Preparation: You'll need three large, uninflated, good-quality balloons and a permanent marker. On the balloons, write the word "me." Before the message, ask three older children to help you. Explain that they'll need to intermittently blow up balloons and hold them shut until you give them a signal to let the balloons go.

Today we're going to learn something about pride. What is pride? Let the children respond. **God wants us to care about who we are and who he has made us to be, but sometimes we forget that God is who made us. We begin to think we're pretty special. The Apostle Paul warned some Christians a long time ago about pride.** Read the Bible text.

I've asked three children to help us with a little experiment today. I'm going to mention some great things about myself, you kids, and our church; then you can mention some things too. Each time we mention something, our volunteers will each blow up a balloon just a little bigger. Let's see what happens.

As you read the following list of "brags"—or one you create yourself—have the three volunteers blow up their balloons little by little.

I'm the greatest teacher in this city.
I have the most beautiful children—they look just like me!
This church is the best church for miles around.
[Name of child] is the smartest child in the whole world!

Make a few more statements—the more preposterous the better—and encourage the children to join in. With each boast, the balloons and the word "me" will get bigger and bigger.

There is no one in the whole world greater than *me!* Have the volunteers let go of the balloons and let them fly.

Read the Bible text again. **Paul says pride makes us think we're better than we are, but love builds up. God's love builds us up so we can know how dear we are to God and how much God loves us. God gives us so many people to love us—and not just when we're good and kind to others, but even when we're not being the kind of people God wants us to be. God forgives because God loves us!**

In your Children's Active Message today, you'll give thanks to God for who you are.

82

Children's Active Message

Leader Tip

If you don't have access to Polaroid cameras, simply have the children draw pictures of themselves.

Preparation: You'll need a Bible, several Polaroid cameras and film, construction paper, glue, and markers or crayons.

As each child enters, take his or her picture with a Polaroid camera. While the pictures develop, have the children sit in a circle. Read to them 1 Corinthians 3:16: **"Don't you know that you yourselves are God's temple and that God's Spirit lives in you?"** Ask:
- **How can God's Spirit live in you?**
- **How does it make you feel to know that God's Spirit lives in you?**
- **If you had a wonderful house, how would you treat it?**
- **What does that say about how we should care for this wonderful "temple" in which God lives?**

When all the pictures have developed, pass them to the children. Invite the children to make "frames" for their pictures from construction paper. On the top of their paper, help the children write, "[Name] is a temple for God's Spirit." Then have children glue their pictures to the paper, draw frames around their photographs, and decorate the paper with pictures of things they do well—play piano or soccer, read, or even hug, for example. When children are finished and if time permits, ask them to explain their drawings.

Fun Follow-Up Ideas

Have the children show their framed pictures to the congregation. Ask a few volunteers to read what their frames say and explain the drawings. Close with a prayer, thanking God for making his Spirit live in us.

26. Our Big, Big Family

Theme: Family

Suggested Bible Text: "Therefore, as we have opportunity, let us do good to all people, especially to those who belong to the family of believers" (Galatians 6:10).

"I have been reminded of your sincere faith, which first lived in your grandmother Lois and in your mother Eunice and, I am persuaded now lives in you also. For this reason I remind you to fan into flame the gift of God, which is in you through the laying on of my hands" (2 Timothy 1:5-6).

Commentary

The difficulty in speaking of "family" is that one is never sure what it means anymore. In the days of *Leave It to Beaver,* it meant Ward and June, always formally dressed for dinner, and their two charming sons. *The Adventures of Ozzie & Harriet* portrayed the same tight, loving family. Now the families that fill the church pews on a Sunday morning are likely to include

● a single mom, never married, who is raising her child on her own;

● a divorced dad with three children who may or may not have the children in church with him depending on custody arrangements;

● widows and widowers, including some young who are struggling with whether to date or remarry;

● couples living together outside of marriage, knowing that it is not as it should be in the eyes of God or the church, yet afraid or unwilling to make a lasting commitment;

● older couples with their grown children living in their homes; and

● singles in many different situations who can well feel isolated in a church that continues to dwell heavily on themes of "family."

So many different configurations of family come trooping in to worship God on a Sunday morning, and each needs a word of encouragement and hope from God's Word.

Scripture exhorts us to be faithful to one another and to love and trust God. The forms of family may change, but the need for Christlike behavior in relationships within the home is the same.

Christian families have an additional responsibility, which is highlighted by Paul in his words to Timothy. Timothy's "sincere faith" was passed on to him by his grandmother Lois and mother, Eunice. Then God used that faith to spread the good news about Jesus to many.

Christian families are incubators for faith. While the temptation may be to pass the task of Christian education and spiritual development to the "professionals" in the church, the family has the unique opportunity to weave the Christian faith into the very fabric of their children's lives.

Christian families also have an additional resource: the church itself. It is, for many, an extended family—sometimes miles from home—in which adults other than parents enter into mentoring relationships with children. The formal Christian education opportunities are supplemented by times of fellowship, worship, and service. Parents and children together grow strong in character and faith in the community of the church.

Any talk of family must, of course, be sensitive to single people in the congregation. They can rightfully feel excluded by talk of husbands, wives, and children. At the same time, they too may be encouraged to find family relationships in this family of faith and to offer their unique gifts as they share their "sincere faith" with others. Thank God for the family, with its unique challenges and opportunities!

Children's Message

Preparation: You'll need a Bible.

Today we're talking about families. A family is a great gift from God, and everyone has one. Who are some people in our families? Let the children respond. **Let's see how many families we have here. I'd like you to stand and link arms with your sisters and brothers if they're here with you.** Let the children respond.

But our family is bigger than that! All children who are in kindergarten, stand and link arms; now all first graders. Let the children respond, and continue until all children are linked.

Let's have all children who have blond hair link arms; all children with brown hair. Let the children respond, and continue until all children are linked.

Now here's the big, big, biggest family of all: Everyone who loves Jesus, link arms. Let the children respond. **God gives us many kinds of families. Moms and dads and sisters and brothers and all of those other wonderful relatives make up one kind of family, and we thank God for them. But there are other kinds of families as well. Good friends at school are another kind of family. And the big, big, biggest family is our family of believers—all those people throughout the world who love Jesus Christ.**

Listen to what the apostle Paul wrote about our family of believers. Read Galatians 6:10. **Having a family of believers is a wonderful thing, and I thank God that you're part of our family of believers.**

In your Children's Active Message today, you're going to think about your families and how God has made your family special.

Children's Active Message

Preparation: You'll need scissors, construction paper, tape, and markers. Cut several pieces of construction paper into eleven one-inch-wide strips. Each child will need twenty to twenty-five strips.

Say: **Today we're thinking about our families, and each family is different. Some children have many, many people in their families; others have only a few people in their families. Today we're going to think of all the people in our families and some of the special things about them. You'll write a family member's name on a strip of paper; then you'll write a word that describes that person. You'll continue until you've made a strip of paper for each person in your family—including yourself.**

As an example, write your mother's name on a strip of paper, and then write a personality trait such as "kind." Say: **Then you'll tape each strip into a circle to make a family "chain."** Show the children how to make a circle from a strip of paper, and then loop another strip through the first circle to make a chain.

Leader Tip

Have enough helpers present to assist the younger children, asking them the names of their relatives and what is special about them. If the children can't remember, suggest that your helpers write things such as "uncle" or "aunt" on the strips.

Say: **When you're through, you'll have a whole chain of family members' names. Let's get started and see how many family members we can chain together!**

When all the children have finished, say: **In the Bible, Paul tells us that all people who believe in Jesus are like one big family. Let's see how big our family is when we join all our chains together!**

With the adults' help, tape the children's chains together. Stretch the big chain around the room while you remind the children that everyone who believes in Jesus is part of the "family of believers." Close by praying: **God, we thank you for brothers and sisters and fathers and mothers around the world. Help us to love one another as you love us, and help us to look for others to invite into your big, big family!**

Fun Follow-Up Ideas

Have the children proceed into the sanctuary with the large chain of names. If there are not enough children to hold the chain, invite members of the congregation to join the parade. Have one or two children explain that they made a paper family chain that includes the names of their relatives, and that they then joined all their chains together to remind them that everyone who believes in Jesus is like a big family.

You may also want to find a place in the church to display the children's family chain.

27. Who Does It Belong To?

Theme: Stewardship

Suggested Bible Text: "How can I repay the Lord for all his goodness to me? I will lift up the cup of salvation and call on the name of the Lord. I will fulfill my vows to the Lord in the presence of all his people" (Psalm 116:12-14).

Commentary

Why do so many of God's people view stewardship as so painful? Perhaps the reason is that some Christians talk of stewardship only during the period of time when the church is preparing the budget for the coming year. Or perhaps the reason is that we limit stewardship so. We think of it only as giving some money to the church so that the church can stay afloat. Hence, if we can wring a few more dollars out of the faithful, we'll be able to do so much more as an institution.

That's a far different view of stewardship than Scripture presents to us. In the Bible, stewardship is the full range of "rendering" to the Lord what truly *is* the Lord's because of what he's done for us. By creating, sustaining, leading, and redeeming his people, God pours out upon us grace after grace. How do we respond?

In the Old Testament, the tithe, a tenth of one's worldly store, was to be used for God (Deuteronomy 14:22-23). In the New Testament, Jesus helps us see that all we have and are belongs to God, given to us as stewards to tend and keep. To each is given "talents," shares of God's wealth, and we're expected to wisely use what he gives us instead of hiding the talents in the ground (Matthew 25:14-30).

Stewardship is this creative tending of what is God's. When we begin to believe that what we use and enjoy in this world is ours to do with as we please, a delicate balance is destroyed. Witness the ravaging of our natural resources by those who feel that the earth belongs, not to the Lord, but to whoever has the money to purchase land rights! A careful reading of the Bible's first two chapters lets us know that we are stewards of the earth God created, not its owners.

We can teach children that the earth is a gift from God and not *the* god. Children can grow in appreciation of the material order as something they are called to have dominion over, but not dominate. They can hear the first commandment—"You shall have no other gods before me" (Exodus 20:3)— and know that God will provide for their needs with the expectation that they join in this lifelong adventure of providing for others and caring for God's creation. That's stewardship in the best, widest, most scriptural sense.

Children's Message

Preparation: You'll need a Bible, a hole punch, strips of paper, a marker, pieces of string, tape, and a globe. You'll also need to ask parents before the message to bring in various toys, sports equipment, dolls, and clothes. On the strips of paper, write, "Property of _____." Then punch a hole in each strip of paper, and tie a piece of string through each hole.

Today we are thinking about stewardship. What is stewardship? Let the children respond. **Stewardship is taking care of something that doesn't belong to you. Jesus told a story about a rich man who left on a trip and gave his servants part of his riches. The servants who used his riches to make more money were rewarded, but the servant who hid his money was punished. God wants us to wisely care for that which is his.**

But how do we know what belongs to God?

I have some toys and clothing that belong to some of you. If you see something that belongs to you, tell me so we can put a label on each item. Then we won't forget who these things belong to. Show the children each item. As children claim each item, write the child's name on a label, and attach the label to the item.

I guess we've labeled everything. What if I want to put an owner's label on [child's name] **or** [child's name]**? Who "owns" them?** Let the children respond. **Our parents are in charge of us, but we really belong to God.** Write "God" on two labels, and tape the labels to the children.

Show children the globe. **How about this? This is a globe of the whole world. Who does the world belong to?** Let the children respond. Write "God" on another label, and tape the label to the globe. **In fact, all the things we've labeled really belong to God.** [Child's name]**, your dad or mom may have bought this item, but someone somewhere made it out of things that God gave to us.** Read the Bible text. **All the good things we have come from God, and God lends them to us for just a little while to take care of. That's what it means to be a steward. We take care of things that don't belong to us.**

In today's Children's Active Message, you're going to walk around God's creation for a while and help take care of it by picking some things up.

As you go to the Children's Active Message, sing "He's Got the Whole World in His Hands" to remind us that the world belongs to God. Start the song for the children to sing.

Children's Active Message

Leader Tip

If you want to have the children do any planting or yardwork, also provide garden utensils and other necessary supplies that are safe for young children.

Preparation: You'll need plastic trash bags. Before the Children's Active Message, select an area outside the church that children can easily walk around and clean in a short period of time. Be sure to prepare the area by removing sharp objects that might hurt the children.

Say: **Today we are talking about stewardship. Stewardship means that we take care of things that don't belong to us. How do you take care of things that don't belong to you?** Let the children respond, and then say: **God has given us so many gifts in this big world, but sometimes we forget that we are stewards who take care of what doesn't belong to us. Today we're going to take a "stewards' walk." We'll look for things that God has given us and think about how we might take care of those things. We'll also take care of God's world by picking up trash.**

Distribute the trash bags. Then lead the children on a walk outside, asking them about what belongs to God and how they might care for those things. After the walk, ask:

● **What did you see that God has given us to take care of?**
● **Why do you think people don't always care for God's world?**
● **How can we help others to be good stewards of God's world?**

Fun Follow-Up Ideas

Have the children proceed to the front of the congregation with their trash bags. Then have a few volunteers explain what the children found. Ask another volunteer to tell the people how the children decided to help others be stewards of God's creation. Close with a prayer, asking for God to help our efforts as his stewards.

28. Just Start Talking

Theme: Prayer

Suggested Bible Text: "I love the Lord, for he heard my voice; he heard my cry for mercy. Because he turned his ear to me, I will call on him as long as I live" (Psalm 116:1-2).

Commentary

"Teach us to pray," a disciple said to his rabbi, Jesus (Luke 11:1). That is still the passionate plea of God's people who yearn for that natural, powerful conversation with their heavenly Father but may struggle to achieve it. For many, prayer is an element of faith that falls into the "should" category. We *should* be more active in doing God's work; we *should* give more money to the church; we *should* pray more.

When prayer is seen as privilege and possibility rather than as pressure, new joy opens to us. Prayer may seem most natural within a congregation of Christians, where a prescribed order of worship provides structure, hymns stimulate mind and spirit, and the commentary of others—preachers, readers, and other believers—serves to stoke the fires of prayer within. But there are inevitably those moments of silence and solitude when we sit, struggling with thoughts and feelings, pushing aside doubt, wondering whether God really has time for our meager needs when so many others are in worse condition.

Just talk! That's the key! Jesus assumes that when there is a relationship with God, conversation follows. "But when you pray, go into your room, close the door and pray to your Father, who is unseen. Then your Father, who sees what is done in secret, will reward you" (Matthew 6:6). Jesus does not say, "if you pray" because he assumes that those who love God will be talking and listening. God loves us so much that he sent his only Son to suffer and die, so of course he wants to be in constant dialogue with his children. Prayer, then, is a matter of listening and speaking. We listen in quiet, inviting God into the still privacy of our being. We speak, unleashed from carefully guarding our words.

Just talk! As we become more and more aware that God is "turning the ear" to us, our love increases and our need to speak with our loving God becomes a part of our life. But first, just start talking!

Children's Message

Preparation: You'll need a Bible, a children's drum, a pencil, paper, a typewriter, a laptop computer or other small computer, an unplugged telephone, a cellular phone, a pager, and any other communication devices available.

What a wonderful time for us to be alive. There are so many ways to communicate with one another. A long time ago, people used drums to send special codes or special messages. Bang on a drum. **People also wrote messages and sent letters to tell one another what they thought. People also used typewriters.** Let the children push keys on the typewriter. **Now people often use computers to communicate.** Hold up the laptop computer. **We also use telephones** (hold up the telephones) **and pagers** (hold up a pager). **We also use fax machines, and some people say we'll soon communicate through our watches! Whew! What a wonderful time to communicate.**

We have a special way to communicate with God, too. What's it called? Let the children respond. **Prayer needs no plugs, no electricity, no drums, nor even paper and pencil. Prayer comes from inside you. God will always hear your prayers and will answer your prayers, although the answers may not be what you expect or understand. Listen to what the Bible says about prayer.** Read the Bible text.

God wants us to "call on him as long as [we] live." He wants us to pray to him all the time. Today in your Children's Active Message, you're going to offer your prayers to God in letters. Even though we don't need paper and pencils, they can sometimes help us think of what to say. Let's communicate with God in prayer!

Children's Active Message

Preparation: You'll need sheets of lined paper, markers, pencils, and pens.

Ask:

● **How many of you have a pen pal? Could someone explain what a pen pal is?**

Say: **Pen pals are fun because you learn so much about where they** live, and you get to tell them all about your home and friends and what you like to do. Sometimes pen pals even get to visit one another. Pen pals can become good friends. When we have good friends, we want to write them and call them on the phone and be with them all the time. Because God is our friend, God wants us to talk with him all the time. Ask:

● When you pray to God, what do you say?

Say: Today let's pretend that God is our pen pal. Let's pray to God by writing him a letter. You can say anything you want to God. You can ask God questions or tell him about yourself. Let God know about friends who are sick or who you would like God to help. Let's write some letters to God!

Help the children write their letters to God. If time permits, have volunteers read some of the letters to one another. Close by praying: Dear God, we know that we can talk with you any time, all the time. Thank you for always listening to us and answering with love. In Jesus' name, amen.

29. Getting to Heaven

Theme: Salvation

Suggested Bible Text: "We...know that a man is not justified by observing the law, but by faith in Jesus Christ. So we, too, have put our faith in Christ Jesus that we may be justified by faith in Christ and not by observing the law, because by observing the law no one will be justified" (Galatians 2:15-16).

Commentary

It seems so simple: Our access to God and eternal life is not due to anything we do, but is based on what God has done for us through his Son. It is the essential truth of the Christian faith. Yet from New Testament times to the present, Christians have struggled with grace. In Paul's day, the question was whether a Christian was bound to keep the traditions, laws, and rituals of Judaism to have eternal life. The council at Jerusalem (Acts 15) formally settled the matter, but the issue kept returning in individual churches and is troubling even to this day.

Could it be that the message of God's grace seems simply too good to be true? While we know it "in the head," we struggle to live it in our lives. So we continually ask how God could love people as sinful as we are. "What must I do to be acceptable to God?" "How can others who don't have the faith 'credentials' I do possibly go to heaven?" All are questions of entitlement. God answers with grace.

Children learn about God's grace through example and experience. As they live with "grace-full" families who treasure them for who God has made them to be, who encourage them to love others on the same basis, and who freely forgive them when they fall, they grow strong in the assurance of their salvation. We have much to teach—and learn from—the children.

Children's Message

Leader Tip

If you don't have access to a roll of tickets, simply make tickets yourself from construction paper. Don't forget to print "Ticket to Heaven" on each ticket you make.

Preparation: You'll need a Bible, a roll of tickets such as those from party-supply stores, and a marker. Print "Ticket to Heaven" in visible lettering on each ticket.

You'll need enough tickets to make a large, visible cross during the message.

Today let's talk about how we can live with God forever. There once were people who said that to live forever with God, you had to earn it. These people figured that you must have to pay for something as wonderful as living forever with God. After all, when you want to go to the movies or to your favorite amusement park, you buy a ticket. Hold up the roll of tickets, and distribute them to the kids. **You can get into a movie theater with a ticket, but what happens if you don't have a ticket?** Let the children respond.

God is different, though. God doesn't charge us anything for his love. Read the Bible text. **As a matter of fact, God's love for us even cost him a great deal. Let's take our tickets and put them down here on the floor to see what God's love cost him.**

Help children arrange their tickets on the floor in the shape of a large cross. **What did it cost God for us to be able to live with him forever in heaven?** Let the children respond. **Jesus died on the cross so we might know how much God loves us. And when this life is over, we will go to heaven to keep loving God forever.**

You can't buy a ticket to heaven or earn it in any other way. God gave it to you by sending Jesus to die for you. God loves you that much!

Today in your Children's Active Message, you'll do something that will let people know about the wonderful free gift God gives us.

Children's Active Message

Preparation: You'll need paper and pens. Before the Children's Active Message, create "invitations" that include the following statements:

An invitation to _____
to live forever with God in heaven!

"For God so loved _____ that he gave his one and only Son, that whoever believes in him shall not perish but have eternal life" (from John 3:16).

Shared with you by _____ on _____.
                       (Name)   (Date)

Be sure to print the name and address of your church at the bottom. You'll need enough invitations for each child to have one.

Leader Tip

If you have access to a photocopy machine, create one page of invitations; then photocopy the rest.

95

Open by singing a children's song about God's grace—"Jesus Loves the Little Children," for example. Remind the children that we can live forever with God in heaven without paying for it or doing things to earn it. Explain that many people don't know about God's free gift of love and that we need to be reminded of God's gift of love all the time. Ask:

- **What causes us to forget Jesus' love?**
- **How can we remind ourselves of Jesus' love?**

Distribute the invitations. Read through the invitation with the children, and encourage them to think of a friend, brother, sister, parent, or other loved one who they'd like to remind about God's love. In the space next to the words "An invitation to," have each child write the name of the person to remind about God's gift of love; have them each write the name again in the space within the Bible verse. Then have children each write their own name in the space after the words "Shared with you by" and fill in the date.

Encourage the children to give their "invitations" to their loved ones when church is over.